Elementary

BIG BOOK of Science Fun

DAVID C COOK

transforming lives together

BIG BOOK OF SCIENCE FUN FOR ELEMENTARY KIDS
Published by David C Cook
4050 Lee Vance Drive
Colorado Springs, CO 80918 U.S.A.

Integrity Music Limited, a Division of David C Cook
Brighton, East Sussex BN1 2RE, England

ISBN 978-0-8307-7244-5

The content included in this book was originally published in *Fizz, Foam, & Froth Science Lab for Ages 5–7* by David C Cook in 2009 © David C Cook, ISBN 978-1-4347-6724-0; *Fun Science That Teaches God's Word for 6- to 9-Year-Olds* by David C Cook in 2004 © David C Cook, ISBN 978-0-7814-4081-3; and *Fun Science for 10- to 12-Year-Olds* by David C Cook in 2008 © David C Cook, ISBN 978-0-7814-4558-0

Cover Design: James Hershberger
Illustrators: Marilee Harrald-Pilz, Guy Wolek, Brett Lamb, Laurent Renault, Matthew Hertel

Printed in the United States of America

2 3 4 5 6 7 8 9 10 11

091523

Contents

"Me" Matter: Formulating Who I Am

Common Bonds: Transforming My Relationships

Introduction

Slime. Balloons. Goo. Cooking Oil. Water. Really fun stuff for elementary kids—really great teaching tools for you to lead them along the path of discipleship!

The more we understand science, the more we stand in awe of God. Nothing attests to the endless imagination of God like the world He created. Every square foot of the natural world is filled with wonders just waiting to be explored. And the things you and your kids can cook up with just a few supplies will bring new understanding of important spiritual truths right along with the "oohs" and "ahs."

These little scientific wonders will work in your elementary classroom (although middle schoolers may be fascinated by these activities too!). Your kids get to be the scientists, often working in pairs or groups. There are no plans for noxious gases or wall-shuddering explosions, but a sturdy vinyl tablecloth is recommended. After all, you can't make slime without getting a little slimy!

Experiments and the lessons that go with them are grouped according to three themes:

- Properties of God: Discovering Who God Is
- "Me" Matter: Formulating Who I Am
- Common Bonds: Transforming My Relationships

You'll find a clear goal for each activity in the Truth Explosion, along with suggested themes and Scriptures that correlate to the experiment. The Formula for Success lists the supplies you'll need—most of them readily available from your grocery or pharmacy. Think how much fun you'll have watching your sometimes-distracted kids totally engrossed with their experiments and absorbing spiritual truth. Then check the Lab Results for a brief wrap-up discussion and Beyond the Laboratory for an extra, more in-depth activity.

Some activities provide scientific treasures for your kids to take with them. Others can be repeated with family and friends with the kids in the teaching role, flaunting their scientific prowess and making the application to how we live as followers of Christ.

So what are you waiting for? Grab your goggles and white coat—the lab is all yours!

Leading a Child to Christ

One of the greatest privileges of serving in children's ministry is to help guide children to become members of God's family. Pray and ask God to prepare the kids you know to understand and receive the good news about Jesus. Ask God to give you the sensitivity and wisdom to communicate effectively and to be aware as opportunities occur.

When talking with children about salvation, use words and phrases they understand; never assume kids understand a concept just because they can repeat certain words. Avoid symbolic terms that will confuse literal-minded thinkers. As you watch and pray, you will see kids developing relationships with God.

Here are some questions you can ask and things you can discuss with a child who is interested in accepting Jesus as their Lord and Savior. Encourage the child to look up and read the Bible verses along with you.
Read John 3:16. **Why did God send Jesus to earth?** (God loved us so much that He wants us to have eternal life with Him.)

First John 3:1 says that God wants us to be His children. But sin, doing wrong, separates us from God. Read Romans 6:23. **What do you think should happen to us when we sin?** (die) **But what is God's gift to us?** (eternal life in Jesus)

Jesus willingly died on the cross to take the punishment for our sins. Read 1 Corinthians 15:3. **But Jesus didn't stay in the tomb. After three days, He came back to life! Jesus died so that we can live forever in heaven with Him.**

Are you sorry for the wrong things that you've done? If you are, what should you do? Read 1 John 1:9. **Our sins are wiped away when we're truly sorry for what we've done and when we turn to God.**

Read Ephesians 2:8. **How are we saved?** (by God's grace, through faith) **Christian faith is a life-long adventure here on earth. With Jesus as Lord of our lives, we build a life of submitting to God, following Jesus, and keeping in step with the Spirit.**

At this point, continue to talk with the child about accepting Jesus as Lord and Savior. Include what your church teaches about how this happens. If you have any questions about salvation, talk with your pastor or children's ministry leader.

God wants every person to accept the free gift of eternal life that He's offering. What do you need to do about this?

Every Bloomin' Thing

Topic: Creation
Time:10–15 minutes
Group Size: Individuals
Mess Meter: 1 **2** 3

For everything God created is good.
—1 Timothy 4:4

Truth Explosion: God created everything.

Formula for Success

- paper cups (1 per child)
- white sidewalk chalk (1 piece per child)
- brown markers (not permanent)
- water
- 1 seed

Use this activity to remind kids God created a beautiful world for us. Evidence of His love is all around!

Begin this experiment with a question about growing plants. **How do you grow a plant?** (put a seed in dirt, water it, put it in sunshine, etc.) **Can you grow a plant without a seed?** (no) **When God created plants, He just spoke! He told the ground to grow plants, and it did! We can't just tell the ground to grow plants, but we can do an experiment that will help us understand what it might have been like when God created plants.**

With a brown marker, draw a line around a piece of chalk about two inches from one end. **We can pretend this line is the ground.**

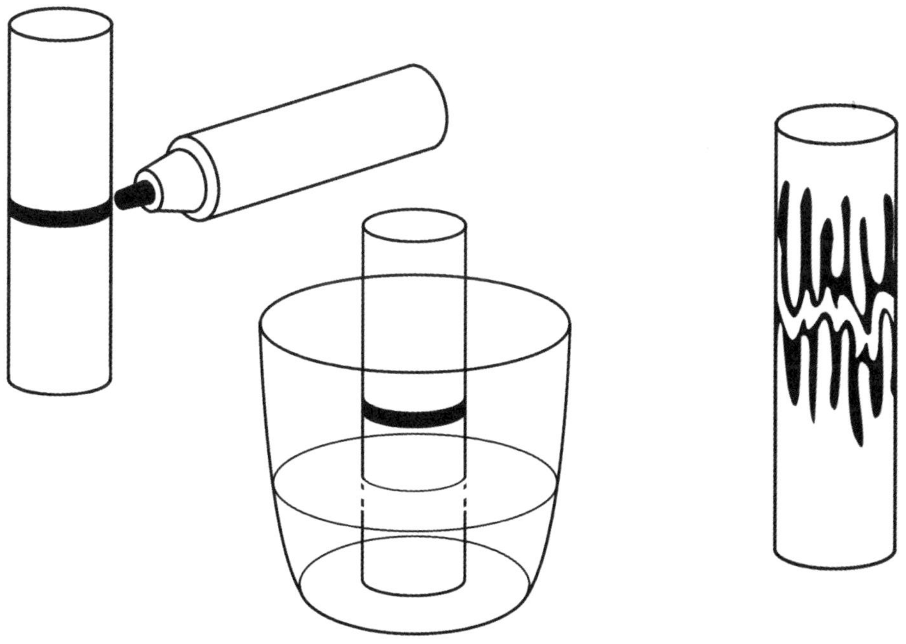

Genesis 1:11–12; 2:9

Note: Different brands of markers, even of similar shades of a color, may produce different results. If you like, try a variety of brands ahead of time to see which brown marker works best.

Pour about one inch of water in the bottom of each cup. Place the chalk in the water so the line is above the water. **Now let's tell flowers to grow from the ground. Say it all together: "Grow!"**

It will take a few minutes for the chalk to absorb the water. Play a short game of "Hide the Seed" while you wait. Have each child take turns hiding a seed while the other kids look for it. Say "green" when kids are close to the seed and "brown" when they're farther from it.

After a few moments, look at the chalk. **The brown line has moved up the chalk in shades of pink, orange, and yellow! Wow! It looks like our flowers grew!**

Lab Results

- **What are some of the plants and flowers God created?** (trees, bushes, roses, etc.)
- **How did God "make" plants?** (He spoke and the plants grew.)
- **Why did God make such a beautiful world for us?** (because He loves us so much)

Super Science Fact

Brown ink really isn't brown—it's a mixture of many different colors. Ink gets its color by absorbing some of the colors in white light and reflecting others. When all these colors are combined, many colors are absorbed, leaving very little to reflect. Water is a solvent for water-based pigments. As the water spreads through the chalk, the pigments in the marker dissolve and we can again see all the colors. This process is called chromatography.

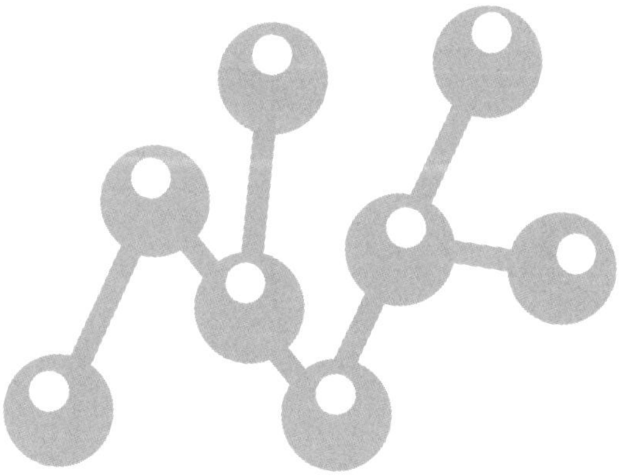

Beyond the Laboratory

Truth Explosion: God created everything.

God's creation is amazing! Choose the correct response to complete each of the following statements:

1. Although polar bears have fluffy white fur, their skin is actually ___________.

   pink **black** **white**

2. Unlike humans, ____________ sleep while standing up.

   pigs and turtles **chickens and ducks** **horses and cows**

3. Despite its name, the killer whale is actually a type of ____________.

   dolphin **shark** **jellyfish**

4. The ____________ land mammals on Earth are elephants.

   smartest **largest** **rarest**

5. _________ lions are actually the best hunters.

   Male **Sick** **Female**

6. Venus is the ____________ planet in our solar system.

   hottest **biggest** **farthest**

7. ___________ is the coldest place on Earth, with a recorded temp of -126.9 degrees.

   Alaska **Antarctica** **Alabama**

8. ______________ actually moves faster uphill than downhill.

   Fire **A black bear** **Rain**

9. Glass is made from ______________.

   water **diamonds** **sand**

10. Earth has 45,000 _________________ every day.

    thunderstorms **earthquakes** **blizzards**

What is your favorite part of God's creation? What makes it your favorite? Say a prayer thanking God for His wonderful gift of creation, and for His unending love for each of us.

Answers: black, horses and cows, dolphin, largest, Female, hottest, Antarctica, Fire, sand, thunderstorms

Ye Old Wizer Geyser

Topic: Faithfulness
Time:15–20 minutes
Group Size: Small groups
Mess Meter: 1 2 **3**

And whatever you do, whether in word or in deed, do it all in the name of the Lord Jesus, giving thanks to God the Father through him.
—Colossians 3:17

Formula for Success

- small glass jar with screw-on lid
- medium nail
- hammer
- drinking straw
- modeling clay
- straight pin
- bowl
- hot and cold water
- tablecloth

Use this activity to remind kids that God is a geyser of faithfulness—He always provides and never lets us down. Our loving response should be up to the task!

Truth Explosion: God is faithful to us.

Spread the tablecloth on your worktable as you speak to your group. **Who has heard of the hot water geyser called Old Faithful?** Pause for responses. **Old Faithful is a geyser found in Yellowstone National Park. A geyser is an underground spring that spurts a tall tower of heat and hot water every few hours. This particular geyser is named Old Faithful because it is faithful, always spurting on schedule. Park rangers—and visitors—can depend on the geyser to spray and amaze.**

Today let's make a geyser to help us remember God wants us to be as faithful as that famous geyser in living the way He taught us.

Depending on the size of your class, you may wish to have several groups make separate geysers.

Fill the jar with cold water three-quarters full. Use the hammer and nail to poke a hole in the jar lid. Push a straw through the hole and screw the lid on the jar. Make sure the bottom of the straw is in the water. To seal off the opening, press modeling clay around the straw where it meets the lid. With another piece of clay, plug the top of the straw. Use a pin to make a hole through the clay plug. This

Genesis 6:9—8:22; Numbers 13:1–2, 17–30; 14:6–9; Matthew 1:18—2:12

is where the water should come out. **Let's see. Everybody ready?** Set the jar in a bowl of hot water and stand back. Expect a shower!

God is faithful to us. He wants us to be faithful to Him by making choices that show others what God is like.

Lab Results

- **How can a geyser help us understand what it means to be faithful?** (by remaining the same, even when other things change)
- **Tell me some other words for *faithful*.** (*dependable*, *reliable*, *trustworthy*, *constant*)
- **Why is it important for us to be faithful to God in the way we live and the choices we make?** (because other people can learn about God by watching us)

Super Science Fact

As the water warms in the jar, the air molecules inside move faster and farther apart. This "excited" state of expansion causes the water to move and burst from the straw.

Beyond the Laboratory

Truth Explosion: God is faithful to us.

Many things and people in our lives are faithful, but many are not! Read each item listed below and decide whether it is FAITHFUL or NOT FAITHFUL.

1. An alarm that only works part of the time	**FAITHFUL**	**NOT FAITHFUL**
2. A friend who talks behind your back	**FAITHFUL**	**NOT FAITHFUL**
3. The sun that comes up every morning	**FAITHFUL**	**NOT FAITHFUL**
4. A teacher who always helps you	**FAITHFUL**	**NOT FAITHFUL**
5. A bus that is sometimes very late	**FAITHFUL**	**NOT FAITHFUL**
6. A dog who sometimes licks you and sometimes bites you	**FAITHFUL**	**NOT FAITHFUL**
7. An ice cream shop that sometimes serves you spoiled milkshakes	**FAITHFUL**	**NOT FAITHFUL**
8. A grandparent who always listens	**FAITHFUL**	**NOT FAITHFUL**
9. A parent who has never missed one of your soccer games	**FAITHFUL**	**NOT FAITHFUL**
10. A friend who suddenly ditched you for a new group of friends	**FAITHFUL**	**NOT FAITHFUL**

Nobody's perfect, and people will always mess up and let us down. But we can always count on God to be faithful to us. Check out these Scriptures that tell about God's faithfulness. Then choose your favorite and memorize it this week!

- Lamentations 3:22–23
- Psalm 36:5
- Psalm 86:11

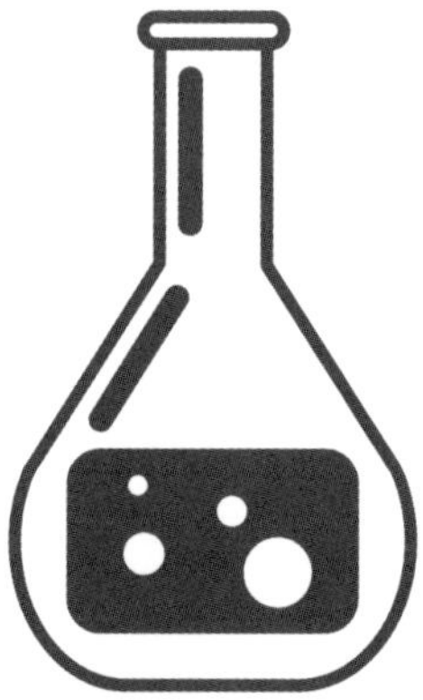

Choices, Choices

Topic: Wisdom
Time: 20 minutes
Group Size: Individual
Mess Meter: **1** 2 3

For the Lord gives wisdom; from his mouth come knowledge and understanding.
—Proverbs 2:6

Formula for Success

- plain paper
- pencils
- small classroom items, such as glue sticks, small jars, hole punch, scissors, paperback books, and erasers

Can your kids stand the pressure? Make simple pencil holders and discuss the benefits of wise choices.

Truth Explosion: God is wise.

Hand out sheets of paper and pencils for kids to use.

Let's get right to the point (hold up your pencil) **of our lesson today. Pick up your paper and see if you can stand it in such a way that it will hold your pencil. In other words, make your plain sheet of paper into a pencil holder!** Allow kids a minute or two to work. Undoubtedly, you'll have kids who will bend and shape their papers to fashion one-of-a-kind pencil holders. Good for them!

Good thinking! As you may have discovered, paper without any folds cannot take the weight or pressure of even a simple pencil. Without our wise God, we cannot stand up for what we believe in and make wise choices. We'd be on our own, falling flat—like many of our pencils did! But because God is wise, we can be wise too! His Word teaches us how to live in a way that honors Him, and we do that by making wise choices.

For those kids who haven't figured it out yet, show them how to fold the paper in half lengthwise. Then starting at the short end, accordion-fold the paper.

Now place your pencil holder on the table and place your pencil proudly on top! **Sometimes it's hard to stand up under pressure. It isn't easy to make the wise choices God would want us to—but when we count on God to help us, we can do it!**

Have kids pair up. Set out the small classroom items. **Take turns with your partner and talk about the peer pressure you face in the lunchroom or on the bus after school. How well do you stand up? As you share stories, pick an object and place it on your "pencil holder." See if it can take the pressure.**

Genesis 13:1–17; Numbers 13:1–2, 17–30; 14:6–9; Daniel 1:1–20

Lab Results

- **What kinds of things do friends say that hurt your feelings?** Answers will vary.
- **In what ways do friends help you make wise choices?** (They help you think about what can happen as a result of a choice; they listen to your feelings; and so on.)
- **If God hired you to manufacture a gizmo that would help kids resist peer pressure what would it look or sound like?** Answers will vary.

Super Science Fact

This paper stand is surprisingly sturdy. As origami enthusiasts know, folded paper derives its strength from its structure and construction.

Beyond the Laboratory

Truth Explosion: God is wise.

Proverbs are wise sayings that offer advice about how to live your life. Read these old English proverbs and try to match each proverb with its correct ending.

Two wrongs don't make a	**the worm.**
You can't judge a book by	**throw stones.**
People who live in glass houses shouldn't	**wait.**
Good things come to those who	**its cover.**
A picture is worth a thousand	**right.**
Two heads are better than	**words.**
The early bird catches	**one.**

The Bible is full of proverbs too! In fact, one entire book of the Bible is devoted to proverbs written by King Solomon. Solomon asked God to give him the gift of wisdom to rule God's people, and God granted his request. Look up the following proverbs and write them in your own words.

Proverbs 17:17 ______________________________

____

Proverbs 3:5 ______________________________

____

Proverbs 1:8 ______________________________

____

Proverbs 8:11 ______________________________

____

Answers: right, its cover, throw stones, wait, words, one, the worm.

Mambo Milk

Topic: God's provision
Time: 10–15 minutes
Group Size: Individuals
Mess Meter: 1 **2** 3

Trust in the LORD forever, for the LORD, the LORD himself, is the Rock eternal.
—Isaiah 26:4

Formula for Success

- aluminum pie plates (1 per child)
- milk (not skim)
- liquid food coloring
- dishwashing liquid
- cotton swabs (2 per child)

Use this activity to help kids understand that because God cares for them, they have nothing to fear.

Truth Explosion: God cares for us.

The Psalms are beautiful poems and songs that praise God. In Bible times, they were used in worship, just like they are now. In Old Testament times, some people would sing and dance to praise God. Let's do a beautiful experiment that will remind us of a beautiful psalm. There might even be some dancing in our experiment!

Pour milk into each pie plate until it's about one-half inch deep. Put two or three drops of each color of food coloring into the milk, but DON'T STIR IT.

Give each child a cotton swab. Have students dip a cotton swab into dishwashing liquid. **Put the end of your cotton swab gently on the milk, but don't stir. Now, lift your swab out of the milk, dip it in some more dishwashing liquid, and then put it in a different place in the milk. Watch the food colors dance!**

This is a really pretty experiment, and students will probably want to play with it more. As they do, recite a simplified version of Psalm 23:

The Lord is my Shepherd.
He gives me all I need.
He gives me rest.
I will not be afraid.
He loves me.

Lab Results

- **The Psalms were written to praise and worship God. How do you like to praise and worship God?** (singing, dancing, clapping, jumping, etc.)
- **Think about the words in Psalm 23. David praised God because he could trust God to care for him. What can we trust God to do?** (We can trust Him to give us what we need, to take care of our families, to keep us safe, to love us, etc.)

Super Science Fact

All liquids have something called surface tension. It's the tendency of liquids to want to pull together at the center. Look at a drop of water. Have you noticed that the edges seem rounded up like a bead? That's surface tension! Milk contains fats. Liquid dishwashing soap is specially designed to disperse fat, which lowers the surface tension of the milk immediately surrounding the dishwashing liquid. This causes the surface of the milk to move away from the dishwashing liquid, taking the food coloring with it.

Beyond the Laboratory

Truth Explosion: God cares for us.

Unscramble the letters to fill in the missing words from Psalm 23.

The Lord is my ____________________, I lack nothing. **[PESEHRDH]**
He makes me lie down in green _________________, **[PRSTUASE]**
he leads me beside ______________ waters, **[QETUI]**
he refreshes my soul.
He guides me along the _____________ paths **[RGITH]**
for his name's sake.
Even though I walk
through the darkest valley,
I will fear no __________________, **[LIVE]**
for you are with me;
your rod and your staff,
they ___________________ me. **[TRCOOFM]**
You prepare a ________________ before me **[BLATE]**
in the presence of my _________________. **[SEENMEI]**
You anoint my head with oil;
my _____________ overflows. **[PCU]**
Surely your goodness and love will follow me
all the days of my life,
and I will dwell in the _______________ of the Lord forever. **[OSHUE]**

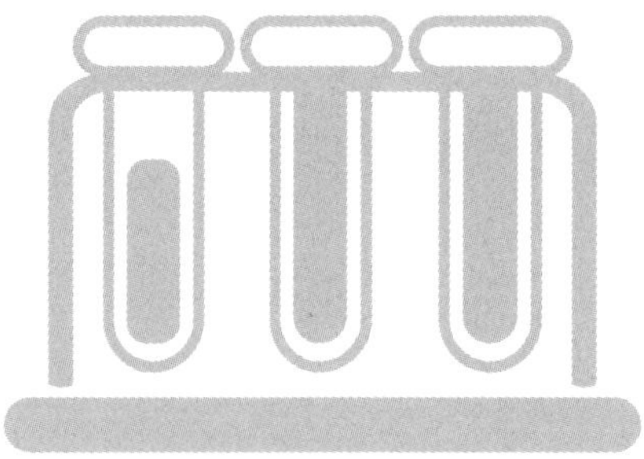

God's Thunderbolts

Topic: God's judgment
Time: 15–20 minutes
Group Size: Small groups
Mess Meter: 1 **2** 3

For God will bring every deed into judgment, including every hidden thing, whether it is good or evil.
—Ecclesiastes 12:14

Formula for Success

- metal cooking sheet (or tray)
- plastic garbage liner (polyurethane)
- modeling clay
- long metal object, like an old-fashioned key or rod

The Old Testament is filled with descriptions of God's strength and dominion over the universe. The biblical writers often describe thunder and lightning as a witness to His infinite power. During this activity, kids will create a tiny thunderbolt in a darkened room.

Truth Explosion: God's judgment is real.

Lightning can fascinate and even frighten anyone who sees its dramatic flash across the sky. While we can't recreate the drama of such a display, we can duplicate the principle at home. In the Bible, God's power is often compared to lightning, and the word picture is obvious: God's power is awesome, so much so that it causes us to tremble.

Crash! Crackle! **Lightning strikes and you run for cover! Lightning scares me a little bit—how about you? I don't know which is worse, the zig-zag flash crackling across the night sky or the loud boom that follows a few seconds later. Either way, it's easy to see why people have always been fascinated by the power of lightning.**

We can't make a huge thunderbolt like the ones God creates, but we can make our own mini-storm with the principles of electricity.

Job 37:2–5; Psalm 97:4

Lay a piece of polyurethane plastic on a table and put the metal tray on top of it. Press a big piece of clay onto the center of the tray. You will use the modeling clay as a "handle," since your bare hand might transfer the electrical charge away from the metal.

It is much easier to see your tiny thunderbolt in a dark room, so turn off the lights and pull down the shades. Rub the tray across the top of the plastic for about 30 seconds. Using the clay as your handle, lift the tray slightly off the plastic at an angle. Keep one corner fairly close to the table.

Bring the key or metal rod close to the edge of the tray. You will see a tiny "thunderbolt" leap from one metal object to the other!

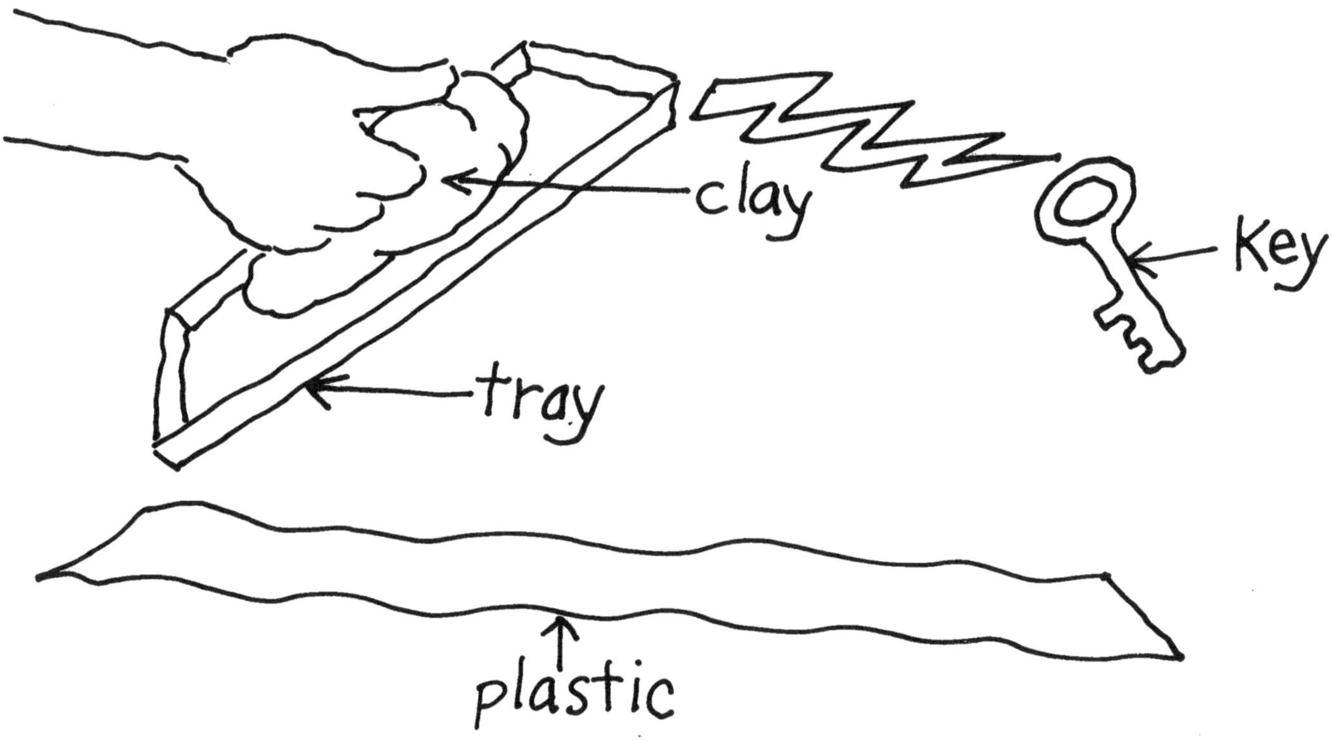

Lab Results

- **When a negative charge and a positive charge touch each other, a spark of electricity is created. Do you know which kind of charge we created with the tray?** (We created a negative charge by rubbing against the plastic. The piece of metal has a positive charge.)

- **We talk a lot about God's love, but the Bible also tells us God is to be feared. Why is fearing God important too?** (Nothing can compare to God. We should respect His power and judgment.)

- **How does lightning remind you of God's power? What do they both seem to have in common?** (You can't mess around with lightning—you have to respect its deadly force. God's power is something we should take seriously too.)

Super Science Fact

Lightning happens when a spark jumps between a negatively charged thundercloud and the positively charged ground. Rubbing the tray against the plastic creates harmless static electricity.

Beyond the Laboratory

Truth Explosion: God's judgment is real.

1. Check it out! In the book of Job, the main character realizes he doesn't have any control over what God decides to do. He speaks about God's HUGE power in this poem. Look up the verses of Job 37:2–7 and figure out what goes in the blanks.

"Listen! Listen to the roar of his voice,

to the _______________ that comes from his mouth.

He unleashes his _______________beneath the whole heaven

and sends it to the ends of the _____________.

After that comes the sound of his ____________;

he thunders with his _______________voice.

When his voice resounds, he holds nothing back.

God's voice thunders in _____________ways;

he does great things beyond our_________________.

He says to the_____________, 'Fall on the earth,'

and to the_________ __________, 'Be a mighty downpour.'

So that everyone he has made may know his ______________,

he stops all people from their ______________."

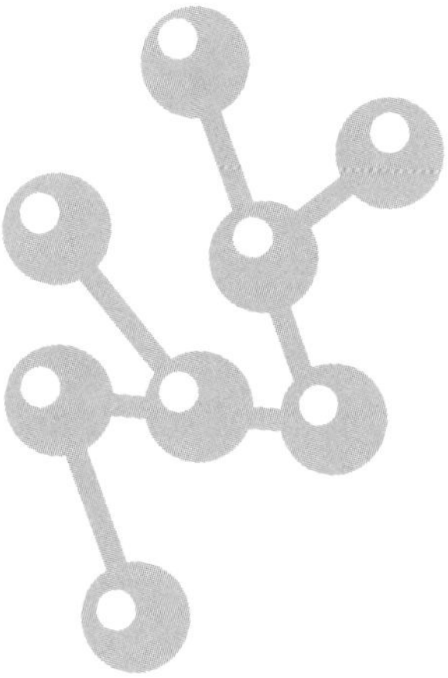

2. In Psalm 97, David lets us know about God's strength:

"The LORD reigns, let the earth be glad
let the distant shores rejoice.
Clouds and thick darkness surround him;
righteousness and justice are the foundation of his throne.
Fire goes before him
and consumes his foes on every side.
His lightning lights up the world;
the earth sees and trembles."

Some of these words are hard to understand. What do you think these words mean? Ask your teacher if you're not sure:

Righteousness	Justice
Foes	Consumes

Afraid of Shadows?

Topic: God's presence
Time: 15–20 minutes
Group Size: Small groups
Mess Meter: **1** 2 3

And surely I am with you always,
to the very end of the age.
—Matthew 28:20

Formula for Success

- lamp with no shade—only a bare bulb
- globe

Even when it feels like God's on the other side of the world, Earth's rotation teaches us that His light is never far away.

Truth Explosion: God is with us even when we can't see Him.

It is natural for us to accept as truth the things we can see. It is not so easy to have faith in things that are sometimes hidden. Show kids the effect of light and shadows on a globe, and they can better understand God's eternal presence in their lives.

Does anybody know what time it is right now in Ethiopia? What about Italy? New York City? (Let students take some guesses.) **The truth is that even though it's _______ o'clock right here in _____________, other people around the world might be working, just waking up, or even snoring in the middle of the night!**

If you've never studied Earth's rotation before, imagine this: even when the sun goes down tonight, it is shining brightly on another country on the other side of the world. Amazing, huh?

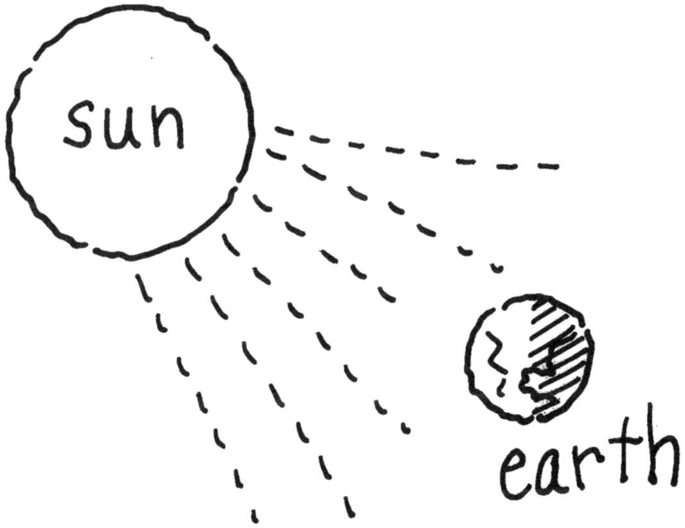

Today we're going to figure out how the sun shines on the world—and learn something about faith in the process.

This experiment works best in a darkened room. Set up a bare lamp bulb on a desk or table opposite a globe. Before you turn off the room lights and switch on the lamp, have your kids pick countries from different parts of the globe. They will be watching the shadow the light creates on these countries as you slowly turn the globe.

As the light shines on the globe, begin to turn it slowly. Students will see the shadow patterns created by Earth's movement.

Lab Results

- **Why was your country sometimes in the light and sometimes in the shadow?** (It depended on whether it was facing the light or not.)
- **When your country was in "darkness," had the light really disappeared?** (The light was just temporarily hidden even though we couldn't see it.) **How is this a little like having faith in God?** (God is still there even when we can't see Him. We might be in darkness sometimes, but the light will again return.)
- **What are some of the things that cause our lives to be "dark"? Does God ever want us to be in darkness?** (Sometimes it's dark because we turn our backs on God. Other times we might be going through a trial that will help us grow. Either way, we know He is present even when the sun seems to disappear.)

Super Science Fact

Earth's orbit is not quite a circle. It is a slightly flattened—or elliptical—shape.

Beyond the Laboratory

Truth Explosion: God is with us even when we can't see Him.

Ask your teacher to help you find out what the times are for some cities around the world. Start with the state you live in, and then draw the correct times on the clocks below.

City: ______________ City: ______________ City: ______________ City: ______________

Time: ______________ Time: ______________ Time: ______________ Time: ______________

Many of the Psalms are beautiful poems written about the nature and character of God. In the space below, draw some pictures of what the writer was trying to express in this poem:

Where can I go from your Spirit?
Where can I flee from your presence?
If I go up to the heavens, you are there;
if I make my bed in the depths, you are there.
If I rise on the wings of the dawn,
if I settle on the far side of the sea,
even there your hand will guide me,
your right hand will hold me fast.
If I say, "Surely the darkness will hide me
and the light become night around me,"
even the darkness will not be dark to you;
the night will shine like the day,
for darkness is as light to you.
—Psalm 139:7–12

I'm Not Afraid of Needles!

Topic: God's constancy
Time: 15–20 minutes
Group Size: Small groups
Mess Meter: 1 2 **3**

Guide me in your truth and teach me,
for you are God my Savior, and my hope
is in you all day long.
—Psalm 25:5

Formula for Success

- wine cork (or small, rigid foam ball)
- broad needle
- bar magnet
- dishwashing liquid
- shallow pan of water

Building a simple compass demonstrates that no matter where we are, a consistent direction will always help us find our way home.

Truth Explosion: God doesn't change.

It's easy to build a simple compass, but not always so easy to follow directions. Before you start this experiment, make sure you know which direction is north.

Imagine you had to find your way across a strange town without any maps, Internet service, or global positioning systems (GPS). You couldn't even ask a gas station attendant! Well, Christopher Columbus not only had to get across town, but had to sail to a foreign continent across the ocean with no maps at all.

What do you know about Christopher Columbus? Accept responses. **One thing we know is that Columbus used a compass to navigate his way across the ocean. Today we're going to build our own compass using a needle and a magnet to help us find out something about finding a fixed point.**

Magnetize a large needle by rubbing it several times in the same direction against the end of a strong bar magnet. You can ask a volunteer to help you.

Psalm 18:30; Proverbs 4:11–14

Push the needle through the rigid foam ball or tape it to a cork. Place a drop of dishwashing liquid in a shallow pan of water. Float the needle in the water, adjusting it horizontally to start.

The needle will start to move. When it stops, which way does it point?

Lab Results

- **How did the compass know it should point north?** (Earth's magnetic field pulled the magnetized needle.)
- **Besides sailors, who else can use a compass to guide the way?** (Hikers and outdoorsmen can use a compass to direct their paths.)
- **How is Jesus Christ like a compass?** (We can look to Him as a "fixed point" or a reference for the way we live our lives. God's words give us direction and they never change course. If we follow Him, we will stay pointing in the right direction.)

Super Science Fact

Earth's core circulates molten iron and nickel—which explain some of the Earth's magnetic pull.

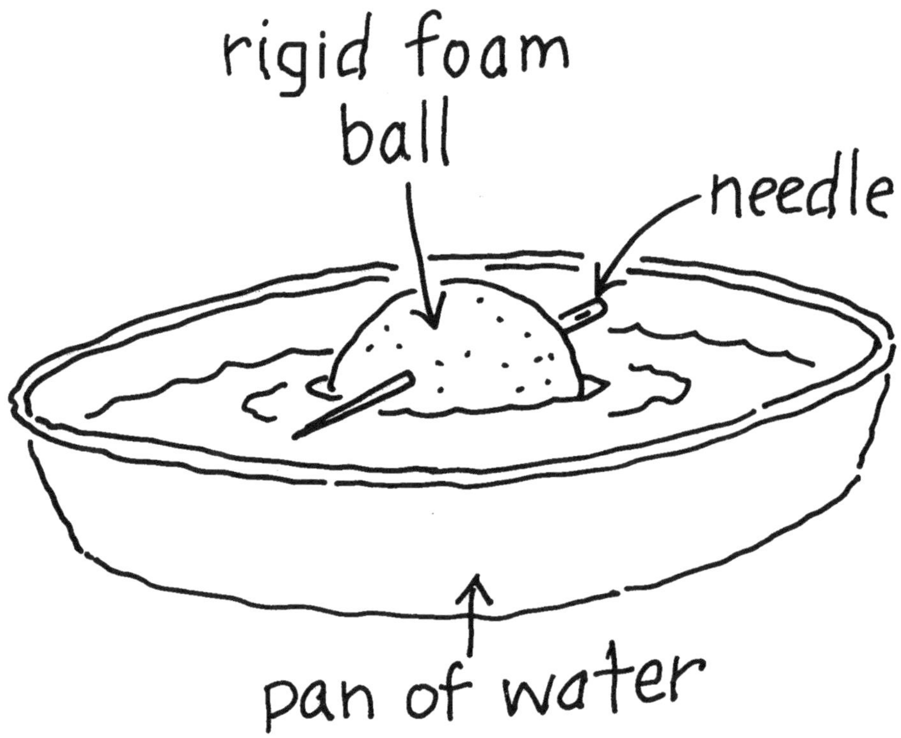

Beyond the Laboratory

Truth Explosion: God doesn't change.

Search for the clue words in the map then fill in the blanks below.

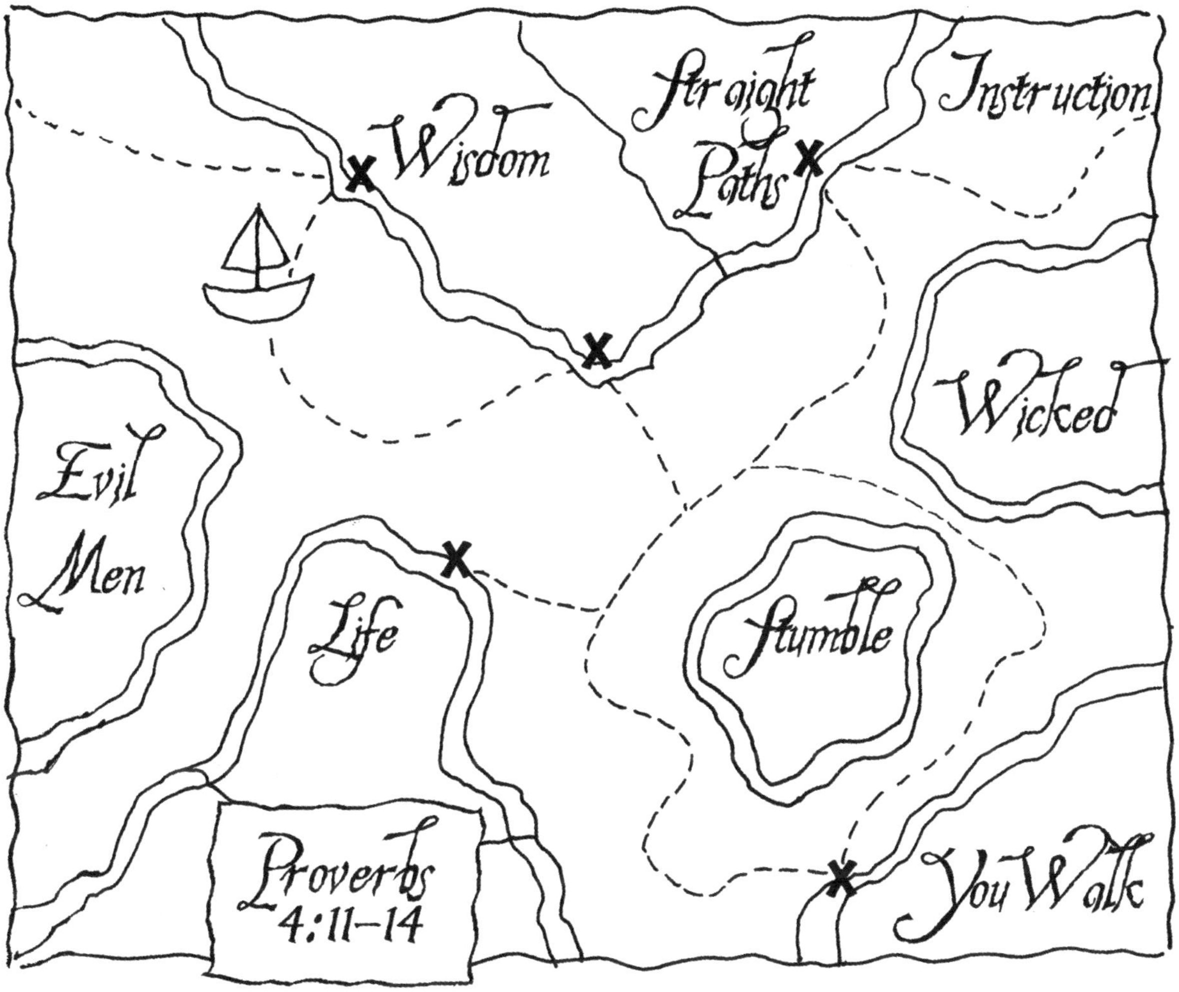

"I instruct you in the way of ________________
and lead you along ________________ ________________.
When ________________ ________________, your steps will not be hampered;
when you run, you will not ________________.
Hold on to ________________, do not let it go;
guard it well, for it is your ________________.
Do not set foot on the path of the ________________
or walk in the way of ________________ ________________."

—Proverbs 4:11–14

Thar She Blows!

Topic: God's amazing ways
Time: 15–20 minutes
Group Size: Small groups
Mess Meter: 1 **2** 3

He performs wonders that cannot be fathomed, miracles that cannot be counted.
—Job 5:9

Formula for Success

- roll of toilet paper
- broomstick
- leaf blower

Ever felt the power of a tornado? A roll of toilet paper can demonstrate the power of gale-force winds with a little ingenuity. With the right power behind it, a small object can become a mighty big force.

Truth Explosion: God's ways are amazing.

Believe it or not, a leaf blower can generate wind force of up to 150 miles per hour—well into the hurricane range on the Beaufort scale. Having this kind of power right in your garage is likely to capture the most bored kid's imagination!

This experiment requires some clean up afterward, but most kids will enjoy chasing after the giant flying streamer created by this activity.

Have you ever heard of "storm chasers"? These guys and gals are just wild! They hop in a truck, grab the video camera, and chase down tornadoes at the first sign of a funnel cloud. Like I said—wild. Why are people so fascinated by the power of a tornado? Listen to answers. **Would you ever want to be a storm chaser?** Kids can share their thoughts.

We're going to see the power of the wind demonstrated by a little machine some of you might even have in your own garage at home. Instead of blowing around leaves and dust—or worse—we're going to blow on a roll of toilet paper and see what happens!

Remind kids that leaf blowers aren't toys and should never be pointed at someone's face. Take your group outside and have a volunteer hold the broomstick horizontal to the ground. Slide the roll of toilet paper onto the stick with a few sheets unrolling over the top and hanging down. The person holding the leaf blower should aim the air stream so it rushes over the top surface of the roll. The hanging sheets will begin to flare up and the roll will quickly unfurl, creating a flying "banner"—a visual testament to the wind's power.

Lab Results

- **Why did the toilet paper soar so high and fast during this experiment?** (The wind created by the leaf blower was more powerful than the flimsy sheets of tissue.)
- **What would have happened if we had used a bolt of heavy fabric or other sturdier material instead of tissue paper?** (Other material would have to be quite heavy to resist the power of the wind.)
- **How are we a little like tissue paper compared to God's power?** (By ourselves, we are fragile and weak. God's power transforms us into something spectacular!)
- **How does God show His power every day in the world around us?** (His power is shown in nature, such as powerful oceans and majestic landscapes. He also shows His power in the way He changes people's hearts and reshapes lives.)

Super Science Fact

The Bernoulli principle describes how air pressure under a moving object pushes it upward. This principle is used in airplane engineering. A plane's wings are shaped so that the air on the top of the plane moves faster than the air underneath.

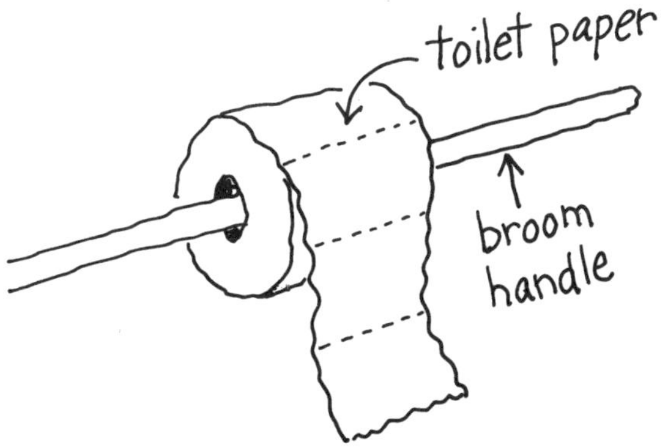

Truth Explosion: God's ways are amazing.

Fill out the chart below with examples of our weakness and God's strength.

OUR WEAKNESS	GOD'S STRENGTH
Isaiah 40:30	Exodus 14
2 Corinthians 12:10	Isaiah 40:28–29
Psalm 49:12	Job 5:9–11

Just for Fun:

Make some paper airplanes that demonstrate the principle of air pressure. How well does yours fly? Have a contest, awarding the farthest-flying airplane with the grand prize.

You can even see what happens when a leaf blower helps "push" your airplane through the atmosphere. Check it out!

Zap! Can You Charge My Battery?

Topic: Strength from God
Time: 15–20 minutes
Group Size: Small groups
Mess Meter: 1 **2** 3

The Lord is my strength and my shield; my heart trusts in him, and he helps me.
—Psalm 28:7

Formula for Success

- lemon
- 2 pieces of wire with ends exposed
- penny
- nickel

Truth Explosion: God gives us strength.

Make a homemade battery using the acid from a lemon and the metal found in everyday coins. Your primitive battery won't have much power, but it will generate enough of a current to create a tingling sensation on the tongue.

I'll bet right now you have some old toys full of dead batteries stuffed in the back of your closet. Am I right? Let kids share their examples. **Some batteries can only be used once, but others can be recharged. Have you ever recharged a battery?**

Batteries aren't magic. Most contain metal plates and strong acid, and this creates an electrical current. With the right ingredients, we can demonstrate how a battery works—and even get a little charge out of it.

Cut two slits about the size of a coin into a lemon. Push a penny and a nickel into the openings. Take two wires and slide the exposed ends in the lemon by each coin. Hold the free ends of the wire to a brave volunteer's tongue. **What does it feel like?**

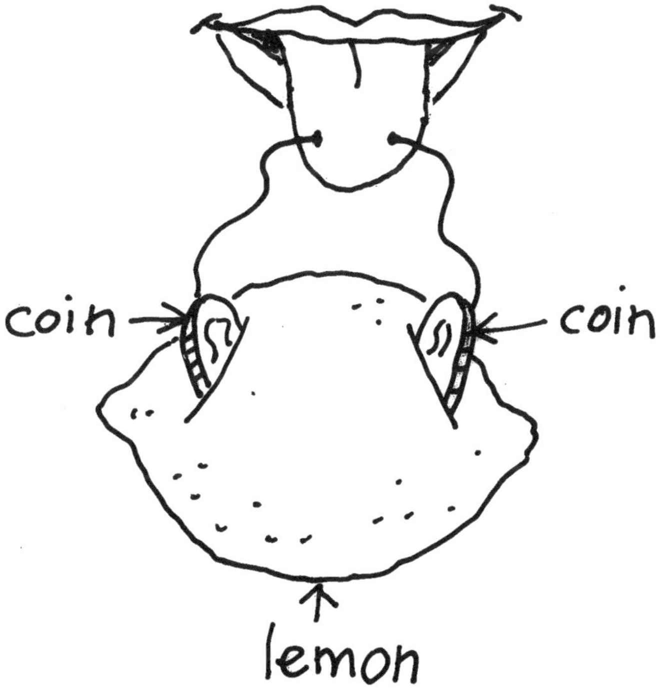

Lab Results

- **Did our homemade battery create much power?** Allow for answers. Have a volunteer who did the experiment discuss what it felt like on his or her tongue.

- **It's not uncommon for us to run out of battery power when we're feeling weary or discouraged. How can we recharge our spiritual batteries?** (We can pray for God to strengthen us. We can spend time with God's people, listen to encouragement from others, or read some of God's promises from the Bible.)

- **Sometimes we get recharged by helping other people instead of focusing on our own problems. What are some things you do to reach out to encourage your friends?** Listen to answers.

Super Science Fact

Most household batteries use a dry cell technique. The inside of the battery contains a paste of electrolytes. Car batteries are more powerful, using wet cells full of sulfuric acid.

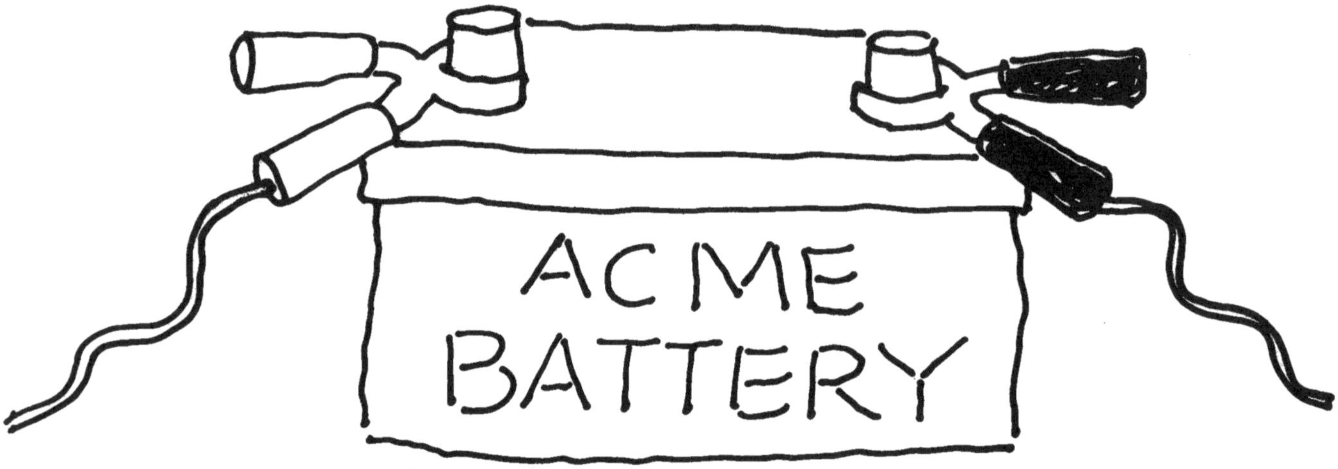

Beyond the Laboratory

Truth Explosion: God gives us strength.

The Bible is full of great promises that can charge us up when we're feeling discouraged. Look up the following verses, and write down the promises God gives us. Have a friend help you!

- Isaiah 40:29
- Jeremiah 31:25
- Matthew 11:28
- Genesis 15:1
- Hebrews 13:5
- 1 John 1:9
- Psalm 84:11
- Romans 8:28
- Isaiah 41:10

Have Water, Will Travel

Topic: Diligence
Time: 20 minutes
Group Size: Large group or small groups
Mess Meter: **1** 2 3

Then choose for yourselves this day whom you will serve ... as for me and my household, we will serve the Lord.
—Joshua 24:15

Formula for Success

- paper towels
- scissors
- green, felt-tipped pens
- glasses
- water
- clothespins

Watch out for blue skies and sunny dispositions as your kids discover that no matter what the future brings, God will be there to help.

Truth Explosion: God helps us.

If you have a large class, you may want to set up several areas for smaller groups to work.

When you serve the Lord, anything is possible—even when things seem impossible to you. God is available to help yesterday, today, and all our tomorrows. When the water rises and trouble appears ready to wash over us, let's choose to serve the Lord and wait for His goodness and mercy.

Cut a paper towel into two-inch strips. On your strip of paper towel, color in a large green dot about two inches from the bottom. **This will be the "eye" of the storm that appears on our troubled horizon.**

Fill the glass about one-fourth full of water. Distribute clothespins. Hang your strip in the glass so the colored dot or "eye" is about an inch above the water. Double-check to make sure the end of your paper towel strip is also in the water. Secure strips with the clothespins.

Let the experiment stand for 15 minutes.

Return to find that the water will have traveled into the thousands of tiny space pockets between the paper towel fibers and advanced upward. Surprisingly, the spot is gone from the paper towel! In its place the paper has turned blue and above that a bright yellow.

While we are busy worrying and wringing our hands, God is at work in our lives. The eye of the storm is gone and on the horizon appears only blue skies and plenty of sunshine!

Although not every problem ends with sunny skies, when we serve God we have the help we need when the clouds build. Remember to serve God with a faithful heart no matter what the weather.

Genesis 6:1—9:17; Joshua 3:1—4:24; 2 Kings 22:1–13; 23:1–6, 21–23

Lab Results

- **When is it difficult for you to choose to serve God?** (when I want to do something different; when I'm afraid or alone; when I am angry)

- **In what ways do you want God to help you this week?** Answers will vary.

Super Science Fact

As water is drawn upward into the paper, so is the green ink. If time permits, try this experiment with other colors. Colors made up of one color pigment will travel much faster than those colors with two or more.

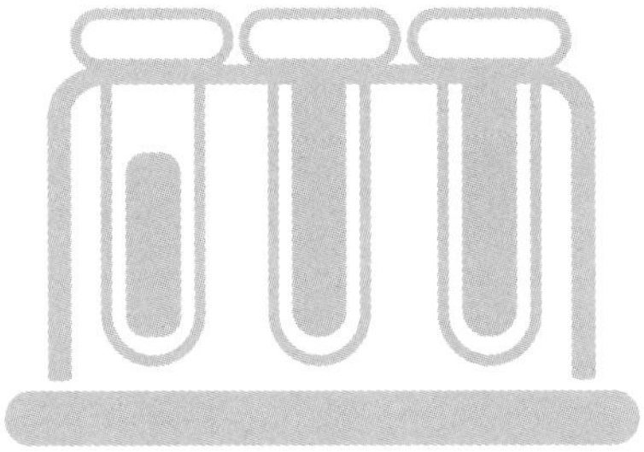

Beyond the Laboratory

Truth Explosion: God helps us.

Look up the following Scriptures and unscramble the letters to find the missing words.

Psalm 46:1
"God is our ________________ and ________________, an ever-present help in trouble."
GRFEEU **TSRETGHN**

Isaiah 41:10
"I am your God. I will strengthen you and ________ you. I will ____________ you with
PLEH **DLPUHO**
my righteous right hand."

Hebrews 4:16
"Let us then approach God's throne of __________ with confidence, so that we may
CARGE
receive _________ and find grace to help us in our time of need."
RMCYE

Acts 26:22
"But God has helped me to this __________ day; so I stand here and ______________ to
YRVE **TTYFSEI**
small and great alike."

How can these verses help you serve God faithfully and with confidence?

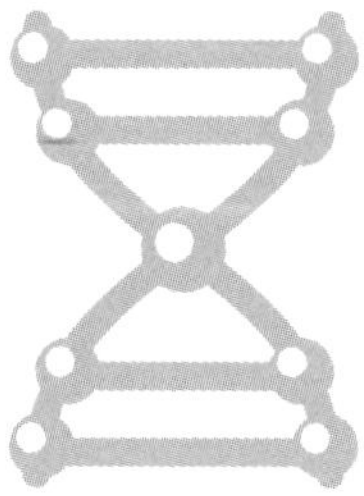

What specific problem are you facing with which you need God's help?

What have you learned today that will help you?

Egg-cellent Protection

Topic: God's protection
Time: 10 minutes
Group Size: Individuals
Mess Meter: 1 **2** 3

And the child [Jesus] grew and became strong; he was filled with wisdom, and the grace of God was on him.
—Luke 2:40

Formula for Success

- brown eggs (1 per child)
- large bowl or dishpan
- disinfectant wipes and paper towels

Children face many dangers today. Help them understand that God protects them no matter where they go.

Truth Explosion: God protects us.

Manage the mess! Although it should be difficult to break an egg if it's squeezed as instructed in this lesson, there's still the potential for a mess. This experiment should be done over a bowl or dishpan, and disinfectant wipes and paper towels should be on hand to clean "eggy" hands.

Brown eggs typically have stronger shells than white eggs. Make sure the eggs don't already have small cracks.

Start this experiment with a conversation. **What does *fragile* mean?** (breakable) **What does *strong* mean?** (not easily broken, powerful) **Do you think an egg is strong or fragile?** (fragile) **If I had something I could squeeze really hard without breaking it, would it be strong or fragile?** (strong) **Now, would you believe me if I told you that you could squeeze an egg really hard without breaking it? Let's try!**

Have students hold an egg lengthwise (small end pointing up) in the palms of their hands. Make sure they hold their hands over a bowl or dishpan—just in case!

Have them gently fold their fingers over the egg (one hand only). Tell them not to squeeze until all their fingers are folded around the egg as much as possible.

Squeeze! Did the egg break? God has given eggs great protection by covering them with strong shells. God protected baby Jesus too!

Lab Results

- **A shell protects an egg. What does God provide to protect you?** (my parents, my home, clothes, police officers, etc.)
- **How did God protect and take care of the young boy Jesus?** (He sent an angel to Joseph to warn him to go to Egypt.)

Super Science Fact

An egg breaks easily when you tap it on something, but it is difficult to break when you squeeze it. The reason is pressure! Tapping the egg against a hard surface applies uneven pressure to the eggshell, causing it to break. Squeezing it applies even pressure along the length of the egg. Most things can stand even pressure, while uneven pressure will cause them to break.

Beyond the Laboratory

Truth Explosion: God protects us.

Just like the egg in our experiment, we can often feel like we are being "squeezed" from every direction. Think about your own life and answer the following questions.

What things do you ask God to protect you from?

How do you feel, knowing God surrounds and protects you?

When something bad happens to you, does that mean God isn't around you?

Why do you think God protects His children?

How can you thank God for His protection in your life?

A Beautiful Covering

Topic: Forgiveness
Time: 15 minutes to do; several days to observe
Group Size: Individuals
Mess Meter: 1 **2** 3

Love your neighbor as yourself.
—Mark 12:31

Formula for Success

- water
- salt (a few cups per jar)
- clear, clean mason jars
- string
- craft sticks (1 per child)
- small pieces of sponge
- wax paper
- tape
- marker (or pen)
- food coloring *(optional)*

Use this activity to teach children that God's forgiveness covers all our ugly sins—over and over and over again.

Truth Explosion: God forgives us.

Note: Try the experiment ahead of time with heated water, not boiling, to help the salt dissolve more quickly and easily. Then try it with room temperature water. Determine which method works best for you. If you use room temperature water, students can add the salt themselves with fewer safety concerns. If using heated water, make the salt solution ahead of time. Use an electric tea kettle if you offer mildly heated water.

Be sure the mason jars are completely clean and dust free. If they aren't, salt crystals may cling to a speck of dust on the side of the jar.

Give each student a mason jar. Write the student's name on a piece of tape and attach to the jar.

Begin the experiment with a question to start kids thinking about forgiveness. **What happens when we don't forgive?** (We stay angry; we hold a grudge.) **What happens when we forgive?** (We can be friends again; we are comfortable around the person we forgave; we don't hurt as much.)

Hold up string and pieces of sponge. **We'll pretend these are our sins. Let's do an experiment to see what happens when God forgives our sins.** Give some students string and craft sticks and give others pieces of sponge. **For those of you who have string, let's get the string ready.** Have kids tie one end of the string around the craft stick. The string should be long enough to be close to the bottom of the jar, without touching the bottom.

Fill the jars partway with water. Instruct kids to pour some salt into the water and stir with their craft stick, but keep the string out of the water. Pour more salt and stir. Continue until no more salt dissolves. **The salt reminds us of what God's forgiveness does with our sins—it removes them so they're gone.**

Encourage students to be patient and persistent in adding salt and stirring. The more salt dissolved in the water, the better the crystals will be in the end.

Add a few drops of food coloring to the salt water if you want colorful crystals.

Place the craft stick across the top of the jar, so the string hangs in the water. If using pieces of sponge, have the kids with sponges simply place them in the bottom of the jar. The sponges will soak up the water and sink to the bottom. **Over the next several days, the salt will form beautiful crystals to cover the string and sponge pieces, reminding us of how God's forgiveness covers our sin.**

Loosely cover the top of the mason jars with wax paper. Then set the jars in a place where they will not be moved. We'll see the beautiful crystals we've created in a few days. As we watch the crystals grow, let's remember God's forgiveness. And let's remember that God taught us to forgive others, just as we've been forgiven so much.

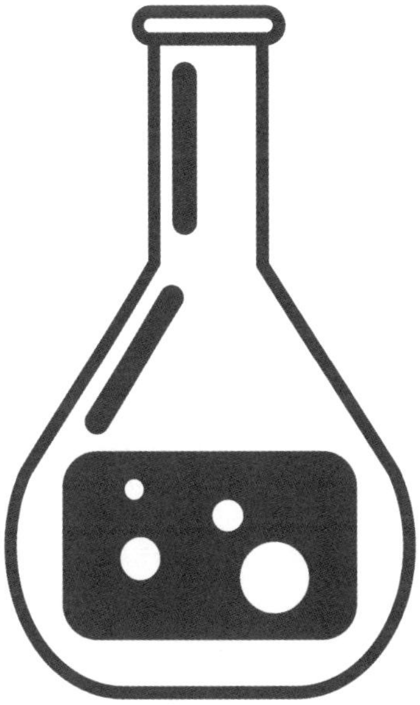

Lab Results

- **What does God's forgiveness do to our sins?** (It covers them. It means God no longer sees them or holds them against us.)
- **When we consider how much God has forgiven us, it makes it a little easier to forgive others. How many times does Jesus say we should forgive someone?** (Keep on forgiving. Don't count how many times you forgive others.)

Super Science Fact

An egg breaks easily when you tap it on something, but it is difficult to break when you squeeze it. The reason is pressure! Tapping the egg against a hard surface applies uneven pressure to the eggshell, causing it to break. Squeezing it applies even pressure along the length of the egg. Most things can stand even pressure, while uneven pressure will cause them to break.

Beyond the Laboratory

Truth Explosion: God forgives us.

Read the following Scripture passages and summarize them in your own words.

1 John 1:9

Psalm 32:1

Isaiah 44:22

Matthew 6:15

1 Peter 4:8

Effervescent Folks

Topic: Worship
Time: 20 minutes
Group Size: Individuals or pairs
Mess Meter: 1 2 **3**

Worship the Lord your God and serve him only.
—Luke 4:8

Formula for Success

- film canisters with snap-on lids (Some camera shops still have these, or you can inexpensively purchase them online.)
- construction paper
- scissors
- clear tape
- effervescent (fizzing) antacid tablets
- pitcher of water
- plastic tablecloth for a launch pad

Truth Explosion: God is worthy of our highest honor, attention, and praise.

Make sure to launch a "Zip-Zop Praise Rocket" before class to see how it operates. Refill it and have it on hand to show your kids. Remember to lay down your tablecloth launch pad before lift off begins.

Zip-Zop Praise Rockets will remind us to praise and worship Jesus our Savior. Have each student make a five-inch wide construction paper tube to fit around the film canister. **Face the open end of the canister downward and make sure it sticks out about one-eighth inch from the bottom of the tube. Securely tape the construction paper tube to the canister. Then cut and accordion-fold construction paper arms and feet and tape them to your tube. Hands reaching upward would be an appropriate posture for worship!**

Pause as kids work. Then hold up a canister lid. Make a little loop of tape, sticky side out, and put it on the inside of the canister lid. Now stick the seltzer tablet to the tape.

Show kids how to pour a little bit of water into the canister—about one-fourth full. Line the kids up for a group launch or let them take turns. When each rocket is ready to launch, snap on the lid (with the attached seltzer tablet). Quickly turn the rocket over and set it on the launching pad. Stand back. Zip-Zop Praise Rockets will zip-zop pop in powerful praise!

There is no one else like God! He's the only one worthy of our highest honor, attention, and praise.

Lab Results

- **What made our little praise rockets really take off?** (They were bubbling inside and the bubbles had to escape.)

- **How are worship and praise like all those excited bubbles?** (If we get excited about God, we can't help but worship Him and tell others.)

Super Science Fact

When the effervescent tablet and water mix, gas pressure builds inside the film canister. When enough pressure builds, the canister blows its top!

Beyond the Laboratory

Truth Explosion: God is worthy of our highest honor, attention, and praise.

You can worship God anywhere, any time, in any number of ways. Use the letters in the word WORSHIP to describe different ways you can show honor, attention, and praise to God.

W

O

R

S

H

I

P

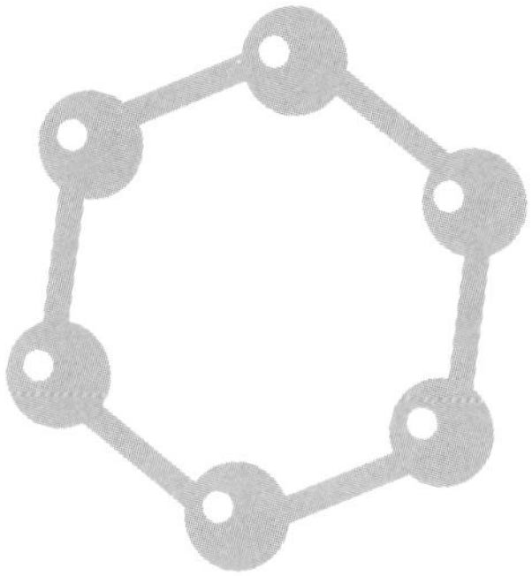

Read Psalm 103. Then use the words in the word box to fill in the verses below.

"Praise the LORD, my soul;

all my inmost _____________, praise his holy name.

Praise the LORD, my soul,

and forget not all his __________________—

who _______________ all your sins

and heals all your diseases,

who ________________ your life from the pit

and crowns you with love and ___________________________,

who ________________________ your desires with good things

so that your youth is _________________ like the eagle's."

Word Box

- forgives
- compassion
- satisfies
- being
- renewed
- redeems
- benefits

Not Sold Separately

Topic: Compassion
Time: 10 minutes
Group Size: Large group
Mess Meter: **1** 2 3

For I am convinced that neither death nor life, neither angels nor demons, neither the present nor the future, nor any powers, neither height nor depth, nor anything else in all creation, will be able to separate us from the love of God that is in Christ Jesus our Lord.
—Luke 4:8

Formula for Success

- a glass filled with water
- powdered fruit drinks (cherry, lime, and grape)
- spoons
- food coloring, bowl, cup, cooking oil *(optional)*

Captivate your kids with swirling color. Use this activity to teach a lesson on compassion.

Truth Explosion: God shows compassion.

Greetings to my favorite bunch of kids! Let's mix a little color today! Place the water-filled glass and powdered fruit drinks where kids can reach. If you wish, substitute food coloring for the powdered fruit drink mixes.

Ask volunteers to use the flat handle of the spoons and scoop up some of the powdered fruit drink and pour it into the glass, one color at a time.

Work slowly, dropping the colors from a height of two inches or more above the rim. The added height causes each color to precipitate—or fall—deeper into the glass. Watch as colors spread throughout the water eventually blending together.

After awhile say, **Oh no. I wanted to do this for the class next door too. Quick. Help me, ______**(fill in with a student's name)**, grab the colors and put them back into the packages. Hurry, please. I can't be late!**

Your kids will look at you like you have two heads. Go with it!

After the looks pass, smile. **Clearly it's impossible to separate colors once they've mixed. And aren't mixed-up days a lot like that? Sometimes we feel like nobody cares and nothing we do will make things better. We started the day a sunny yellow! But somehow it ended up faded and washed out.**

Mark 2:3–12; 6:30–40; Luke 8:40–42, 49–56

Allow a few minutes for kids to share their thoughts and feelings on mixed-up days.

On such days, a hug and smile from a compassionate friend makes things better and brighter. It's also the time for us to remember that nothing, even faded days, can separate us from the love of God. His compassion is easy to get a hold of—just open your Bible!

When we remember that we are never alone, we can show compassion for others who struggle with mixed up days too!

Something Extra!

For another simple experiment in color, pour one tablespoon of cooking oil into a cup. Add three drops each of red, green, and blue food colorings. Mix well. Pour the colored oil into a clear bowl of water. Beautiful! Streams of color appear throughout the bowl.

Lab Results

- **Name times in the Bible where Jesus showed compassion.** Answers will vary, but may include Jesus healing the lepers, forgiving those who crucified Him, or defending the woman caught in adultery.

- **How does God's love turn things around on a gray day?** (It reminds us He has better things in store for us, and He is with us during hard times.)

- **Why is it important that we show compassion too?** (because it helps others learn more about God and His love for them)

Super Science Fact

Sugar crystals (the solute) break apart in water (the solvent). The combination of the two produces a homogeneous mixture known as a solution.

Beyond the Laboratory

Truth Explosion: God shows compassion.

Read the situations below. Circle the answers that best show compassion.

1. There is a new boy at school looking for a place to sit at lunch. You:
 a. keep your head down and eat your food.
 b. invite him to sit with you and your friends.
 c. point out an empty seat at another table.

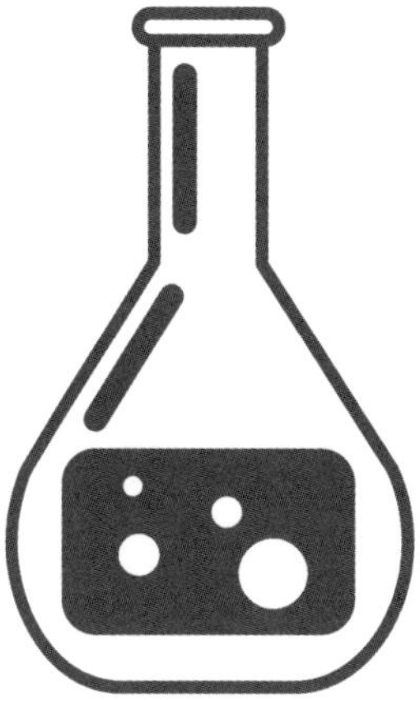

2. Your teacher's mother is very sick and dying. You:
 a. keep your mouth shut. It's none of your business.
 b. find some kind words to say or write to her.
 c. enjoy the fact that she's too sad to assign homework.

3. Your little sister is devastated she didn't make the soccer team. You:
 a. laugh. Come on, she's such a pain!
 b. avoid her. You're sure she doesn't want to talk about it.
 c. give her a hug and offer to help her practice if she'd like to try again.

4. Your dad just lost his job. You:
 a. tell him how much you love and appreciate him.
 b. ask him if you're still getting your birthday presents.
 c. mope around. Misery loves company, right?

Write your own situation and three possible responses:

5.
 a.
 b.
 c.

Say a prayer asking God to help you be compassionate, as He is so others may see His love through you.

Peace and Carrots

Topic: Hope
Time: 10 minutes
Group Size: Large or small groups
Mess Meter: **1** 2 3

Where, O death, is your victory?
Where, O death, is your sting?
—1 Corinthians 15:55

Formula for Success

- glass of water
- salt
- sliced carrot piece
- teaspoon

With some simple items from the kitchen, your kids will get a picture of the resurrection power of God. In it we find peace for life eternal with Him in heaven.

Truth Explosion: God's resurrection power is greater than anything!

When you watch old cartoons, you see characters get smashed over the head with huge boulders or run over by a freight train. They're flattened for a moment then they pop up and run off again. But we all know that's not what happens in real life.

We're careful about a lot of things we do because we know if we get hurt that badly, we could even die. And life is too precious to be careless.

Fill a glass with water. **What do you think will happen if we drop a piece of carrot in this water?** (It will sink.) Ask a volunteer to drop a piece of a carrot into the water and watch it sink.

Is there anything we can do to make that carrot come back up? Jiggle the glass? Blow on the water?

We might say that this carrot has had it. It's not coming back to life, so to speak, no matter how hard we wish it would. We have no power to change it. There's nothing we can do.

But God's power is greater than human power! In the Bible, God's power accomplished amazing things including raising people from the dead. Imagine! Let's say this salt represents God's power.

Ask a volunteer, or several, to add salt to the water a teaspoon at a time. The carrot will suddenly rise to the surface.

2 Kings 4:8–33; Matthew 28:1–10; John 11:1–44

We can celebrate God's resurrection power in our lives. It gives us peace of mind to know God's will for our lives is eternal life with Him in heaven.

If God can raise the dead, then surely He can solve our problems. This same power is at work in our lives. God can do great things.

Lab Results

- **Tell me three words that describe God's power.** Answers will vary.
- **Why is it important to know God's power is greater than human power?** (Because we can know that, no matter what happens, God is in control.)
- **What does "resurrection power" mean to you?** Answers will vary.

Super Science Fact

The carrot is lighter than the denser or heavier salt water, causing it to rise and sit on the water's surface.

Beyond the Laboratory

Truth Explosion: God's resurrection power is greater than anything!

Look up the following Scriptures that tell us about heaven. Then rewrite the verses in your own words.

Revelation 21:4

John 14:2

Matthew 25:34

Revelation 5:13

We don't know a whole lot about what heaven will be like. We do know it will be perfect and holy, a place where we can worship God and experience His love forever. Keeping that in mind, work with a friend to make a list of all the things that will NOT be in heaven. Then look back over your list and talk about how it makes you feel to know that those things are only temporary.

Branching Out

Topic: Depending on God
Time: 15–20 minutes
Group Size: Small groups
Mess Meter: **1** 2 3

Formula for Success

- piece of ivy, grapevine, or a slender tree branch—just cut from its source
- second piece of ivy, grapevine, or branch cut several days earlier *(optional)*
- pocket knife *(optional)*

Without proper connection to its life source, a living thing will die. As young people observe what happens when a branch gets separated from the vine, they will begin to understand the importance of staying grafted into God's kingdom.

Truth Explosion: God is our source of life.

Note: You can do this experiment in two separate sessions with one branch. Kids will observe what happens to the branch when it is cut from its source. If you want to try use two branches—one cut several days ahead of time, the other freshly cut.

Remain in me, as I also remain in you. No branch can bear fruit by itself; it must remain in the vine. Neither can you bear fruit unless you remain in me.
—John 15:4

Take a look at this branch. I just cut it from its tree earlier today. I'm going to pass it around, and I want us to write down what it looks, feels, and smells like. We can even cut into it a little bit to see what it looks like inside.

Let the kids examine the branch carefully, noting its flexibility, color, fresh smell, and water content. If you choose, you can write down your observations in columns on a large piece of butcher paper or a white board labeled ATTACHED.

Now that we know what this healthy branch looks like, let's put it somewhere for a while. When we return together, we're going to compare what happens to our branch after it's been disconnected from its life source.

If you choose to demonstrate the principle in one session, at this point in the lesson bring out the branch cut several days ago. If you're meeting in two sessions, let the kids inspect the original branch, which will be more brittle—snapping easily, drier, limp, or brown in color. Write your findings under the label DETACHED.

John 15:5

Lab Results

- **You all knew our healthy branch would not be able to last very long once it was cut off from its life source. Why? What did it need to stay alive?** (The plant needed to be connected to a root system for water and nutrients.)

- **When Jesus says He is the vine and you are the branches, what is He trying to say? What does a vine have in common with God?** (We are like the little leaves attached to a larger plant. Without God, we can't survive. God is our life source. He creates and sustains us.)

- **How is someone who doesn't know God like the dried-up branch after a few days with no water?** (The person needs to be connected to a source of life in order to grow and be healthy. God is that source.)

Super Science Fact

Grafting occurs when a plant stem or vine is connected and grows into the original host plant. Photosynthesis occurs when light is transformed into energy to help a plant grow and thrive.

Beyond the Laboratory

Truth Explosion: God is our source of life.

Check out this passage from John 15:1–4:

"I am the true vine, and my Father is the gardener. He cuts off every branch in me that bears no fruit, while every branch that does bear fruit he prunes so that it will be even more fruitful. You are already clean because of the word I have spoken to you. Remain in me, as I also remain in you. No branch can bear fruit by itself; it must remain in the vine. Neither can you bear fruit unless you remain in me."

This Scripture uses metaphors, or comparisons, to describe Jesus and His intimate connection with His followers.

1. What makes a vine a good metaphor for Jesus? Think of a couple of good comparisons between the two.

2. What does it mean to "bear fruit"? What kind of actions or attitudes would be compared to good fruit?

3. This verse says that sometimes Jesus has to do some pruning with us. What would pruning look like in your life? Has God ever "pruned" you before? Explain.

Just for Fun:
Plant some grapevines or ivy for your classroom. Include a small stake or toothpick with the following label:

(Your Name) Is Branching Out!
Jesus Is the Vine

Catch Me if You Can

Topic: Confidence
Time: 15 minutes
Group Size: Pairs
Mess Meter: **1** 2 3

Guide me in your truth and teach me,
for you are God my Savior, and my hope
is in you all day long.
—Psalm 25:5

Formula for Success

- unsharpened pencils

With the drop of a pencil, kids will realize how easily confidence turns to doubt and how much they need Jesus to keep their confidence meters high.

Truth Explosion: God is trustworthy.

Hello and welcome! Put on your thinking caps. Today I have a three-part question to start our time together.

Here's part one. How many of you think you could catch a pencil thrown from across the room—using only one hand? Oh, by the way, you're blindfolded. Pause and allow kids to respond. **Not much confidence here!**

Okay. Part two. Suppose I give you permission to remove the blindfold. Could you catch the pencil now? Pause and allow kids to respond. **Hmm. The confidence meter rises!**

Now for part three. How many of you could catch a pencil if I held it right over your hand? (No brainer!) **Let's give it a try.** Have kids pair up. Pass out one unsharpened pencil for each pair of students. Grab a partner yourself and demonstrate the following action. Have your partner position his or her hand as if holding a glass. Hold the pencil 8 to 12 inches above your partner's hand. Have your kids follow your example.

On the count of three, drop your pencils.

(Fun Science Fact: By the time the eye sees the pencil fall and signals the brain, time is lost. Listen as confident hands let pencils fall all over the place!) Switch roles. Some kids will do well with this activity and catch the pencil every time. Have those students decrease (and then increase) the distance between their pencils and hands.

Jesus knows better than we do our strengths and weaknesses. He also knows how quickly our confidence can tumble into doubt. The good news is—and there's so much of it in Jesus!—that Jesus helps us with our doubts.

Jesus will encourage our faith and give us confidence that He is the Son of God. Drop your doubts and catch His confidence!

Matthew 14:22–33; Mark 4:35–41; John 19:1–18; 20:1–8, 19–31

Lab Results

- **What kinds of things do you have the most doubts about? What helps to make you confident? Share some ways to show you are confident in God.** Answers will vary.

Super Science Fact

Gravitation is the force of attraction that exists between all particles with mass in the universe. The force of gravity is responsible for holding objects onto the surface of planets.

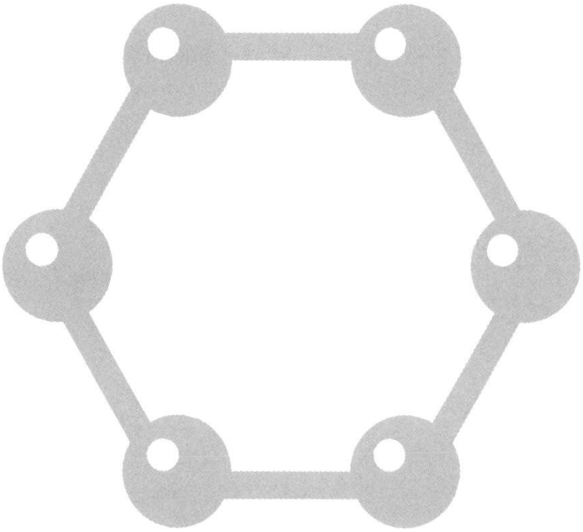

Beyond the Laboratory

Truth Explosion: God is trustworthy.

Finish this prayer in your own words:

God, it's hard for me to trust You when ...

In those times, I want to believe that You ...

Please help me to remember that ...

Give me strength to ...

I ask these things in Jesus' name. Amen.

Read Proverbs 3:5–6 and summarize it in five words or less. Write your summary in the space below.

I'm Just Getting Warmed Up

Topic: Encouragement
Time: 15–20 minutes
Group Size: Small groups
Mess Meter: 1 **2** 3

But encourage one another daily, as long as it is called "Today," so that none of you may be hardened by sin's deceitfulness.
—Hebrews 3:13

Truth Explosion: God wants us to walk with Him.

Formula for Success

- bowl
- boiling water
- 3 spoons: metal, plastic, and wooden
- dried peas or very light beans
- butter

Does going to church make you a Christian? Sitting through a church service won't get you to heaven, but it can heat up your walk with God. Kids discover through the conduction of heat the importance of fellowship.

It's true that church attendance isn't a magic formula for growing in Christ. But we want kids to understand that fellowship with other Christians and good Bible teaching can help to heat up their walk with God. Using three heat conductors (three different spoons) as metaphors, you will help kids observe how their relationship with God can grow with the help of a good church family.

Picture this. You've just taken your favorite jacket out of the clothes dryer. Your mom set the temperature on high, so you're ready to snuggle into its warm, cozy folds, when—OUCH! While zipping up the jacket, you burned your finger on

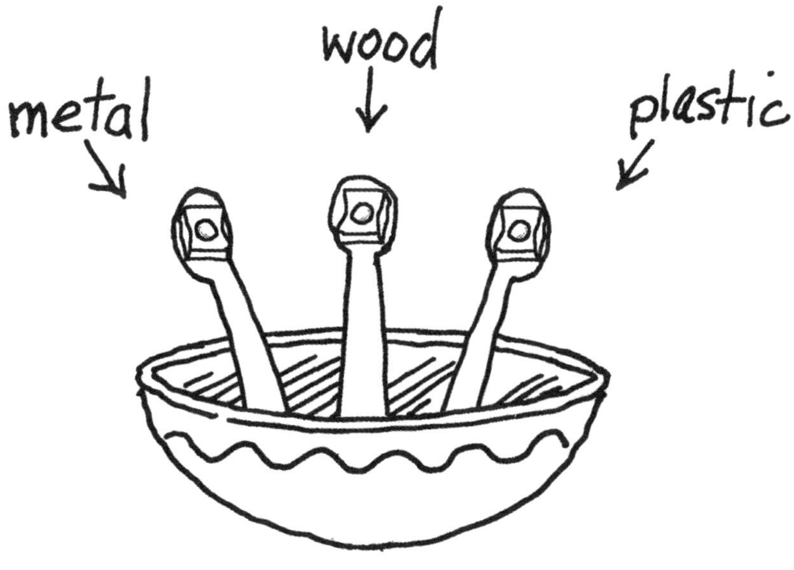

Acts 2:46–47; Hebrews 10:25

the metal zipper. How come? (Metal conducts heat more than fabric. The heat from the dryer turned your ordinary zipper into a tiny, hot iron!) **Let's see if we can test this theory today with some boiling water and a few spoons from the kitchen. We're going to see if heat really does travel faster through metal.**

Carefully pour very hot or boiling water into a bowl resting on the center of a table. Make sure your students do not get close to you while you are pouring. Have three kids place a blob of cool butter on three different spoons—one plastic, one wooden, and one metal. Press a dried pea in the center of the butter until it is slightly anchored.

Lower the spoon handles into the water and let them rest for several minutes. Observe how quickly the peas start to slip down each spoon.

Lab Results

- **Let's imagine our three spoons are three Christians and God is the boiling water. Which spoon represents the person who spends time with other Christians and warms up to God faster? Why?** (The metal spoon. This person is listening to good teaching from the Bible, spends time with other people who believe the same things, and shows discipline and obedience in things like going to church.)

- **How are the plastic or the wooden spoons like other people?** (The other spoons aren't good heat conductors—they are cool toward the things of God. Maybe they don't bother to come to church, or they rarely read the Bible. They don't look forward to hanging out with other Christians.)

- **Most kids can't come to church on their own, but instead they attend with their parents. What if someone's parents don't want to come to church? What can that person do to keep growing close to the Lord?** (Kids can still pray no matter where they are. They can ask Mom and Dad if it's okay to attend church with another Christian friend's family. God understands those situations, and He will still love and support those kids who can't make it to church every Sunday.)

Super Science Fact

Conduction is the movement of heat through solid objects. Metal is a great conductor of heat, but wood and plastic slow down conduction.

Beyond the Laboratory

Truth Explosion: God wants us to walk with Him.

1. What other metal things will heat up more quickly if left in the hot sun?

2. Why do cooks use wooden spoons?

   Why are sleds made out of plastic or wood?

   Why do pots and pans have rubber handles?

3. Look up these verses and write down what the early churches did together:

   Acts 2:46–47

   Hebrews 10:24–25

4. Find a partner. Figure out at least three things you can do to be a good "heat conductor" for God. What will help you "heat up" as a Christian?

Extra Challenge! Write a letter to your pastor or other faithful church worker. Tell this person how much you appreciate how he or she has helped you grow in Christ.

Make No Mistake

Topic: Commitment
Time: 10 minutes
Group Size: Individual
Mess Meter: **1** 2 3

Therefore, if anyone is in Christ, the new creation has come: The old has gone, the new is here!
—2 Corinthians 5:17

Formula for Success

- markers
- strips of paper
- table

Kids will make a few mistakes in this activity—until they learn God's way of doing things.

Truth Explosion: God can change anyone's heart.

Hand out the paper strips and markers, one strip and marker per student. Make sure to keep a paper strip and marker for yourself.

Use your marker to draw a heart on your paper strip. Pause. **That's great. Now on the other side of your strip, write or draw a common mistake kids your age do that makes life harder for others.** A few examples are: gossip, disobeying parents, cheating, and lying.

Now place your paper strip close to the edge of the table like this. Demonstrate for your kids using your paper strip and marker.

Then stand the marker, which represents you, near the paper's edge. The object is to see if you can pull out the paper strip, filled with mistakes, without knocking "yourself" (the marker) over in the process.

You can use both hands but you may not touch the marker. Kids will try various methods but markers will undoubtedly tilt and fall.

We all have mistakes written in our hearts. We can try and try but we can't keep them from tipping us over. But in Jesus we become new creations—forgiven of our bad deeds and harmful attitudes and ready to spread God's Word.

Set markers on top of the paper slips again. **Let's try this a whole new way. God's way!** Hold the end of the paper slip gently in one hand and use the pointer finger on your other hand to give it a swift chop just in front of the marker. This time the markers should stay upright! You may want to practice this a couple of times before class to get it right the first time.

God can change hearts. We won't suddenly be perfect, but we'll have God's help with the choices we make in the future. It's a whole new starting point—make no mistake about it!

Luke 19:1–10; Acts 9:1–28; 13:1–3; 16:16–40

Lab Results

- **How do the mistakes we make tip us over the way our markers fell over?** (They can take us in the wrong direction; they can bring us down and make us feel low.)
- **What happens to mistakes when Jesus comes into our lives?** (We still make mistakes, but God forgives us; we try to be more and more like Jesus.)
- **How have you seen God at work in your life making you a "new creation"?** Answers will vary.

Super Science Fact

Gravity is an invisible force that occurs between two objects. Gravity is the reason the Earth orbits the sun, and the reason the moon orbits the Earth. The moon's gravitational pull on the Earth is what causes the rise and fall of ocean tides.

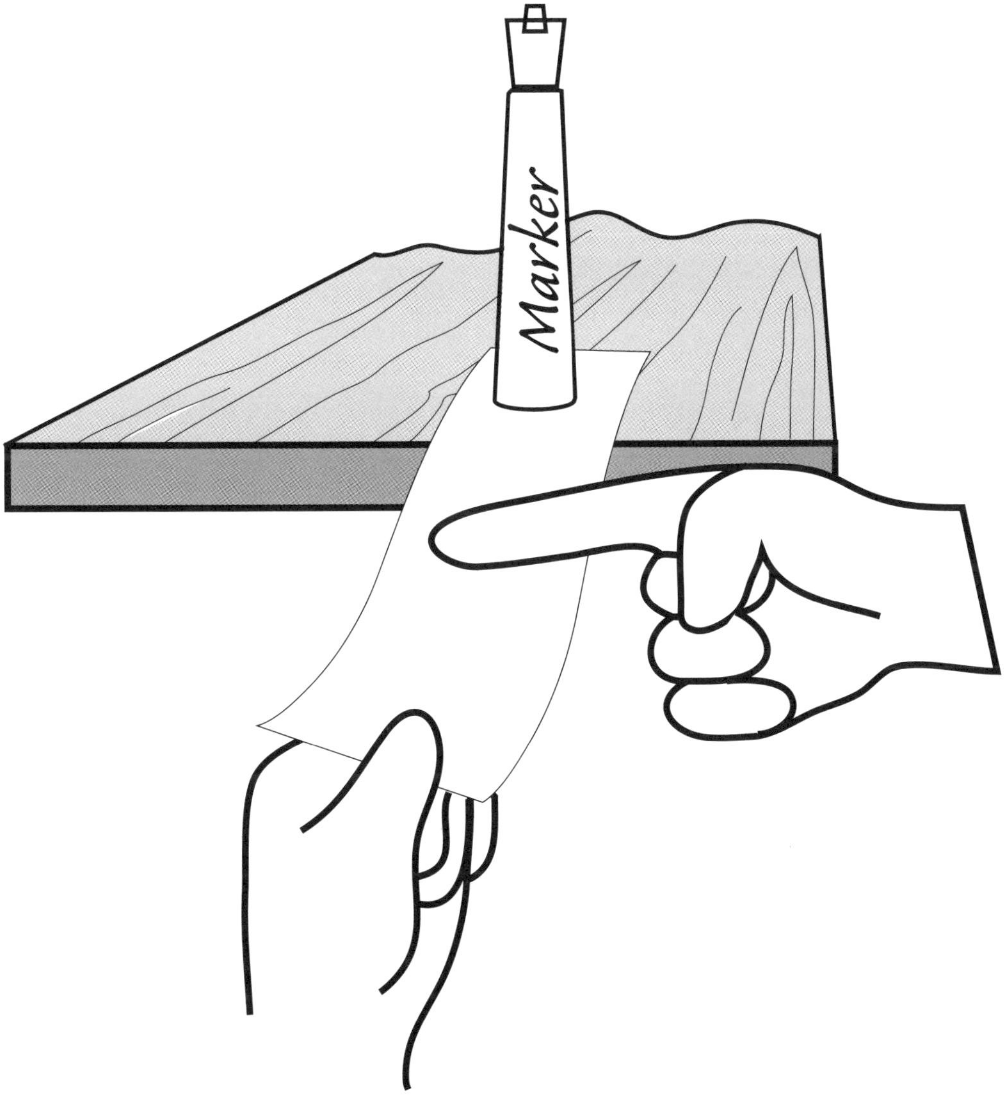

Beyond the Laboratory

Truth Explosion: God can change anyone's heart.

Follow these instructions to discover what God sees when He looks at you!

1. Cross out all the numbers.
2. Cross out all the Is.
3. Cross out all the Xs.
4. Cross out all the Zs.
5. Write the remaining letters on the lines provided.

XPIEO4PZLELOIOZKXATITXHZE6OUXTIWIARXDAPIP8EXAZRA6NCZEXBZU5TTXHEZILOXR9DLOIOZK7SIATXTIH2EH3EZAIRXTZ

____

____

Check your answer in 1 Samuel 16:7.

Lost in the Mix

Topic: Sin
Time: 15–20 minutes
Group Size: Small groups
Mess Meter: 1 **2** 3

Formula for Success

- clear plastic cups
- water
- plastic spoons
- variety of solids and liquids: soap flakes, baking soda, cooking oil, salt, chalk dust, hand cream, fruit juice, or pepper

As hard as we may try to combine them, some things just don't belong together. Kids find out which things in life are designed to blend easily and which things never will.

Truth Explosion: God and sin don't mix.

During this experiment, your group will compare how well some common substances dissolve in water. Before you begin, you might want to put each ingredient into a "mystery" cup or container so your students don't know what each container holds. You might want to label the cups "A," "B," etc., so you can identify the ingredients in the discussion that comes later.

For the wages of sin is death, but the gift of God is eternal life in Christ Jesus our Lord.
—Romans 6:23

All right, are you ready for a test? What do you think happens to a substance when you put it in water? Will it just dissolve and disappear—or will it float around in little pieces? Listen to various answers. **We're going to find out which things blend together easily and which things just can't.**

Ask kids to form groups of four to six. Give each group several cups of water and plastic spoons; then distribute the "mystery" containers. Depending on the number of kids you have, give each group one or more mystery ingredients. Prompt kids to add an ingredient to a cup of water, and then write down what happens to the mixture when they stir. **Here we go. Are you ready to report on your findings? Let's find out which things dissolve in water and which things don't. We are**

Romans 6:22; 2 Corinthians 7:1

going to call one kind of mixture a suspension. This kind of mixture happens when the particles inside the water are bigger than the water molecules. Instead of dissolving, they just float or stay in little pieces in the water.**

The other kind of mixture is a solution. The particles you added are so small they combine into the water completely—almost disappearing! Which side does your mystery ingredient belong to?

You might want to have a large piece of paper or a white board available for recording the substances into two columns, labeled SOLUTION and SUSPENSION. Let each group either report back to you according to the letter on the cup, or you can have a representative come forward and write it on the board.

Lab Results

- **Can you think of any other things we could try to put into water that would dissolve easily?** Answers will vary. **What are some other substances that would just float on top or settle to the bottom?** Answers will vary.
- **This experiment teaches us something about the nature of God. He is so holy that some things just can't exist in His presence—kind of like when we tried to put cooking oil into a cup of water. Why can't God and sin belong together?** (God is completely pure and holy. Sins are dirty and unclean. They don't "dissolve" together, no matter what we do.)
- **What are some things that blend easily with the character of God? In other words, what kinds of things reflect God and His personality?** (When we love each other, pray for forgiveness, worship Him, live clean lives and so forth, these blend easily with God's character. They are part of who He is and how He wants us to live.)

Super Science Fact

A suspension is a mixture in which particles can be seen and easily separated by filtration or settling to the bottom. A solution is a mixture in which both parts combine together completely. Water is sometimes called the "universal solvent" because so many things can dissolve into it.

Beyond the Laboratory

Truth Explosion: God and sin don't mix.

Some of the words in these verses are just too scrambled to make any sense! Blend them a new way and figure out what God wants to tell us about sin and holiness. Rewrite each verse correctly underneath the scrambled verse.

Isaiah 59:2
"But your QUISINITIE have PRASATEDE you from your God."

____

____

____

2 Corinthians 7:1
"Since we have these MOSPRISE, dear friends, let us FYPRIU ourselves from everything that TONCINASEMTA body and spirit, perfecting holiness out of CERVENEER for God."

____

____

____

____

Romans 6:22
"But now that you have been set free from sin and have become VELSAS of God, the benefit you reap leads to NOHLESSI, and the result is NETLARE FELI."

____

____

____

Just for Fun: Write your name in the space below. Scramble the letters to make it tricky for someone to figure out the spelling of your name. (See if you can make a new word out of the letters!)

____

Fold your paper in half. Collect all the names in your group in a basket or hat. Take turns drawing names. As each person draws a name, see how fast he or she can match it to the right person. Who knows? Maybe you'll get a new nickname!

Exposed!

Topic: God's Word
Time: 15–20 minutes
Group Size: Small groups
Mess Meter: **1** 2 3

Formula for Success

- ultraviolet (UV) light (also called a "black light"—available at party or lighting stores)
- tonic water
- glass
- other fluorescent materials such as: mylar, laundry detergent with whiteners, colored chalk, fluorescent paper, parakeet feathers *(optional)*

Just when you think "what you see is what you get," you realize hidden things are lurking in the dark. With the help of a UV light, kids can discover the secrets that might be hiding behind the shadows.

Truth Explosion: God's Word exposes our hidden motives.

Kids love UV lights because they transform ordinary objects into eerie, glowing surprises. That's why fun houses and amusement parks use them and why you will find kids totally drawn into today's experiment.

Your word is a lamp for my feet,
a light on my path.
—Psalm 119:105

Just imagine if all of you walked into this room today with a secret you didn't want anyone to know about. None of us could tell what these secrets were. In fact, from the appearance of things, everything looked normal and perfect.

Let's say on the count of three I could turn on a light switch and suddenly, all your secrets were exposed in big letters across your foreheads! Without warning, we would all know each other's hidden secrets in a flash!

Would you like that? Or would that make you uncomfortable? Listen to kids' responses. **Some secrets aren't that embarrassing or difficult to share—things like the contents of a birthday present or the silly nickname your dad gave you when you were a baby. But other secrets are really personal, and sometimes we want to hide them from the world.**

I'm going to show you a special light called an ultraviolet light. It has certain properties that expose light and color in new ways to our eyes.

Take some tonic water and a clear glass into a dark room. Under normal light, it will appear colorless. But while you pour the water into the glass, shine an ultraviolet light across the stream. It will look like an eerie, luminous stream with a blue glow.

Lab Results

- **Wow! Ultraviolet light is so cool! It can make a lot of ordinary things transform into different colors. Tonic water contains a chemical called quinine that reacts to the UV light. The water seemed so normal—just like regular water—in the everyday light. Just because we couldn't see it, does that mean the quinine wasn't really there in the first place?** (Of course not. It was there all the time, but it took a special light to reveal its secrets.)
- **How are our hearts sometimes like that tonic water?** (We don't always show the outside world our deepest thoughts and motives. We can hide easily in normal light and no one ever needs to know.)
- **Let me read this verse from Hebrews 4:12: "For the word of God is living and active. Sharper than any double-edged sword, it penetrates even to dividing soul and spirit, joints and marrow; it judges the thoughts and attitudes of the heart." How is the Bible a little bit like a UV light?** (The Bible exposes all of our secrets. It shows us where we are wrong and convicts us of sin and deception.)

Super Science Fact

Fluorescence is the process by which UV light (usually invisible) is transformed into visible light. Tonic water contains quinine, whose molecules absorb the energy from the ultraviolet light.

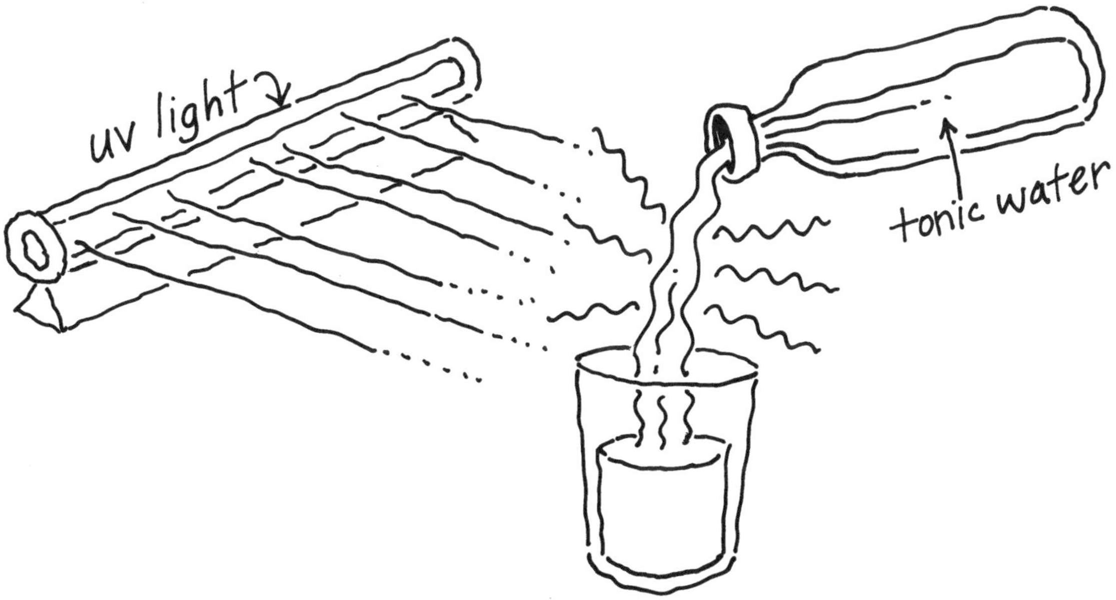

Beyond the Laboratory

Truth Explosion: God's Word exposes our hidden motives.

The word *motive* means the reason behind why we do something. Motives are usually secret, and we are very good at hiding them. The first column contains a situation that might seem really obvious. Place a possible hidden motive in the second column. The first one has been done for you.

EVERYBODY SEES ...	BUT GOD SEES ...
• I am really excited about your new basketball shoes. I tell you how cool they are!	• I am jealous of your great new shoes. I'm mad at my mom for not buying a pair just like them for me.
• I do whatever the popular kids at school want me to do.	
• I do my sister's chores for her, and tell her that I don't expect anything back.	
• I give someone I don't really know a really nice birthday present. Hey—mine is coming up in a few days too!	
• The kid next door asks to borrow my brand new video game for the weekend. I run in and give it to him.	

No Two Alike

Topic: Being made in the image of God
Time: 15–20 minutes
Group Size: Individuals
Mess Meter: 1 **2** 3

Formula for Success

- washable inkpads (various colors)
- transparent tape (a few rolls)
- white paper (1 sheet per child)
- wet wipes
- magnifying glasses *(optional)*

Use this activity to remind kids of their value—of every person's value—in the eyes of God. We are fearfully and wonderfully made in the image of God.

Truth Explosion: I am God's unique creation.

Have wet wipes on hand to clean messy fingertips. Remind students that whatever they touch will leave ink marks, so they should try to avoid touching clothing, walls, etc.

Everything God created is good.
—1 Timothy 4:4

Begin this activity with a conversation with your class. **Did you know that because God made you He knows everything about you? God knows how many hairs are on your head! He can count all your freckles! He even knows about your insides—the parts we can't even see! God made us all different, but we are all made just like Him. Can you tell me something you have that is different from everyone else?** (fingerprints, personality) **No two people in the whole world have fingerprints that are exactly the same! Tiny grooves at the tips of our fingers make our fingerprints. Let's make prints from our fingers to see how they're all different!**

Give each student a different colored inkpad.

Have kids press their index fingers into the inkpad, then stamp the print onto a piece of white paper. If time allows, let students print fingerprints from more than one finger.

Press a piece of tape over fingerprints on the paper to prevent smears and smudges. Be sure kids thoroughly clean their hands with wet wipes.

Have kids trade fingerprint papers with their classmates, then talk about the similarities and differences.

Genesis 1:26–28; 2:18–22; Psalm 8

Lab Results

- **Who is God's special creation?** (People are God's special creation.)
- **What can you do because God made you special?**
  (I can take care of creation; I can learn about God, love God, and talk with Him; I can choose between right and wrong; I can love others and be kind, etc.)

Super Science Fact

Fingerprints are unique! No two are alike, but they can all be put into several different types:

- Arch—a curve, similar to a hill
- Tent arch—a curve that peaks like a tent
- Loop—lines are in a pattern like loops on a shoelace; can be to the right or left
- Double loop—two shoelace loops flopped over each other
- Pocked loop—a loop that goes around a center point
- Whorl—concentric circles or spirals

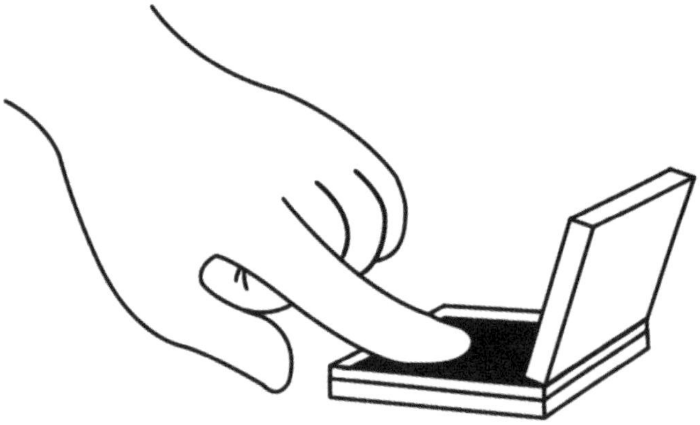

Beyond the Laboratory

Truth Explosion: I am God's unique creation.

Look up the following Scriptures and fill in the missing words.

Psalm 139:14
"I praise you because I am ____________________ and ______________________ made."

Genesis 1:27
"So God created mankind in his own _________________, in the image of God he created them; ____________________ and ___________________ he created them."

Psalm 139:13
"For you created my ________________________ being; you knit me _______________________ in my mother's womb."

Now list three things that are unique or special about you.

1.

2.

3.

Do you see any of these qualities in God? How or when?

Can any of your unique or special qualities help other people learn about God?

Bag O' Trust

Topic: Conviction
Time: 10 minutes
Group Size: Large group or small groups
Mess Meter: 1 **2** 3

So do not fear, for I am with you; do not be dismayed, for I am your God. I will strengthen you and help you; I will uphold you with my righteous right hand.
—Isaiah 41:10

Formula for Success

- zip-top bag filled with water
- sharpened pencil
- candle, match, balloon *(optional)*

Would you trust a bag with a hole in it? Use this activity to show kids that God is 100 percent trustworthy.

Truth Explosion: I can trust God.

Pick up your zip-top bag of water and the sharpened pencil you brought to class. Choose an amiable student and hold the bag over his or her head. Place the sharpened pencil point perilously close to the bag.

Trust. Trust is something that grows alongside love. Babies trust their mothers. Children trust their parents. And students, of course, trust their teacher! Walk around the classroom pausing now and then to hold the water-filled bag above more heads. As you do, ask the following questions:

Can you tell if someone is truly trustworthy? How?

If you were to write a book titled *Trust: Pass or Fail*, what chapter titles would it include?

Set out a large basin or have kids join you at the sink or take a short trip to the water fountain. If you have extra sharpened pencils bring them along. **I need a head, any head. You can trust me!** Have your brave volunteer place his or her head over the sink. Place the bag over his or her trusting head.

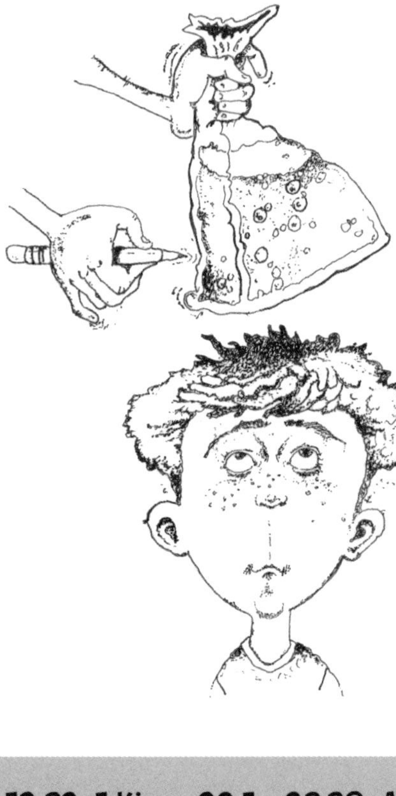

Exodus 6:1—12:32; 1 Kings 22:1—23:30; Acts 7:1–60

Look for a wrinkle-free bulge in the bag. With a twisting motion, push the sharpened pencil point into the bag until you break the surface. There should be no major leaks. Continue to twist until the pencil pokes out the other side. **I told you I could be trusted. A nice, dry head!** Leave the pencil in place. Have kids use extra pencils and bags to give this a try. *Note: Pull out pencils only if you wish bags to drain.*

I'm grateful you trust me. Thank you. But trust can fail miserably in human hands. Feelings like anger, jealousy, and greed will leave us disappointed and upset. But our loving God is 100 percent trustworthy. And because God has helped people in the past, we can trust Him for what's coming up.

Whatever happens, the same God who has been with His people in the past will be with us in the future. Trust Him!

Something Extra!

Fill the bag one-fourth full of water. Place over a candle's flame. Will it break, spewing water all over the place? No! (Fun Science Fact: The heat moves into the water so quickly that the polymer membrane of the bag will not burn.)

Lab Results

- **Name a Bible story that shows God's care.** Answers will vary.
- **Tell about a time God took care of you in the past.** (God healed me when I was sick, helped me be brave when I moved, gives me food and a family, and so on.)
- **What things in your future would you like to trust God to take care of?** Answers will vary.

Super Science Fact

The zip-top bag is made of a chemical compound known as a polymer. When the bag is pierced, the plastic (made of long chains of molecular units) closes around the object, sealing it closed.

Beyond the Laboratory

Truth Explosion: I can trust God.

Read the situations below and think about how easy or hard it is to trust God in each one. Circle your answers.

1. Starting a new school	**easy**	**medium**	**hard**
2. Parents are divorcing	**easy**	**medium**	**hard**
3. Getting a new puppy	**easy**	**medium**	**hard**
4. Family member died	**easy**	**medium**	**hard**
5. Taking a test	**easy**	**medium**	**hard**
6. Friends gossip about me	**easy**	**medium**	**hard**
7. (Write your own idea here) ____________________	**easy**	**medium**	**hard**

Read the following verses. Then choose one to memorize.

Psalm 20:7

Proverbs 3:5–6

Isaiah 12:2

Romans 15:13

Sparkle Rock Geology

Topic: Faithfulness
Time: 20 minutes
Group Size: Pairs
Mess Meter: 1 **2** 3

The Lord is faithful, and he will strengthen and protect you from the evil one.
—2 Thessalonians 3:3

Formula for Success

- rocks
- permanent markers
- liquid starch
- water
- green food coloring
- salt
- small containers for mixing
- small paintbrushes
- shoeboxes
- small greenery

Twinkle, twinkle little rock! Make a sparkling monument diorama that attests to God's faithfulness.

Truth Explosion: I can follow God's leading.

Before class collect enough smooth and clean rocks for your group.

When people wish to remember something important, they often erect a monument or statue. A monument "marks the spot!" For example, think of a large rock that displays the following words: *George Washington Slept Here!* or *Here Lies the Greatest Home Run Hitter of All Time!* Heads turn as people stop to look and remember.

In the Old Testament, Joshua built a remembrance altar. This was a solid stone monument to remind the people of God's help in crossing the muddy Jordan River. It would serve as a reminder to all who came along of God's faithfulness in times past and the days to come. Let's build our own mini-monuments as a way for others to remember God's faithfulness.

Think of how God has been faithful in your life. Ask kids to use a marker and write one or two words on several rocks.

Then have kids pair up and mix batches of sparkly paint. Mix two tablespoons of liquid starch, two tablespoons of water, a few drops of green food coloring, and one-half cup of salt for each pair of students. Use paintbrushes to apply the paint to the rocks. Once dry, this special paint will give your rocks an ancient, mossy look!

Joshua 3:1—4:24; 1 Kings 6:1–17; 8:62–66; Luke 23:32–46; 24:1–12

After the rocks dry completely, have kids stack them in the shoebox to form a monument. Glue "trees" and "bushes" on either side. **Think of other ways you might enhance your memorial diorama when you get home. Share your thoughts with your neighbor.**

God is always faithful. Make it your goal to please Him.

Lab Results

- **How can you learn to stop and listen to God when times get busy?** (I can remind myself of the ways God helps and strengthens me. I can think about what God wants me to do in difficult situations. I can remember how He has helped me in the past.)
- **Name some ways God has been faithful to you.** Answers will vary.
- **Name some ways you can be faithful to God.** (I can talk to Him in prayer and read my Bible. I can make choices that honor and please Him. I can praise Him and tell others about Him.)

Super Science Fact

Geology is the study of the history of Earth as recorded in rocks.

Beyond the Laboratory

Truth Explosion: I can follow God's leading.

In the space below, draw your own monument to God. Think about tough times He has led you through, hard circumstances you are facing right now, and uncertain paths you may face in the future. Use words, drawings, and symbols that remind you of God's love and faithfulness.

If possible, use your drawing as a model for an actual monument. Build it from rocks, wooden blocks, or anything else you choose. Place it in a spot where you will see it every day and be reminded that you can trust God and follow His leading.

Stuck Like Glue

Topic: Faithfulness
Time: 15–20 minutes
Group Size: Individuals
Mess Meter: 1 2 **3**

Greater love has no one than this: than to lay down one's life for one's friends.
—John 15:13

Formula for Success

- disposable cups (2 per child)
- plastic spoons (1 per child)
- Epsom salt
- hot water
- all-purpose glue (not washable)
- 2 teaspoon measuring spoons
- tablespoon measuring spoon
- paper towels
- resealable sandwich bags (1 per child)
- bowls for Epsom salt and water

Use this activity to teach children the value and importance of real and lasting friendships—in a fun and sticky way!

Truth Explosion: I can be a faithful friend.

When first mixed together, the Epsom salt, water, and glue mixture will start to form a blob. Be patient; it's not done yet! Keep stirring and the blob will start to fall apart and take on the texture of ricotta cheese. Now you're done! It will form a blob again when you press it between paper towels. Do not dispose of this mixture down the drain.

Prepare the area by placing multiple layers of paper towels at each student's work area.

Use an activity to help students understand polymers. **What is a polymer?** Kids will probably not know, but let them guess. **It's a mixture where chemicals link together as if they're friends.** Say *polymer* a few times until everyone can say it easily. **Let's play a game to learn about polymers.**

Everyone find a friend and link arms. Now find another group of friends and link arms with them too! Great! We've made a friend chain. Chemicals like to link together to form chains too. Now, let's bend and twist our chain like a bowl of spaghetti. Guide students, moving slowly as one big blob with their arms linked! **Do you think we could move across the room this way? How can we do that?** (by working together) **All right, let's try!** Help kids move slowly and carefully across a part of the room. **Great job! Now let's make a polymer that works in this same way!**

Place bowls of Epsom salt and water on the table within easy reach of the students. Give each student a disposable cup. Have kids scoop one teaspoon of Epsom salt and one teaspoon of water into their cups.

Epsom Salt
Glue

Have kids stir the Epsom salt and water together with a plastic spoon until most of the Epsom salt is dissolved. Give each student a second disposable cup. Let kids measure two heaping tablespoons of glue into these cups.

Now pour your salt and water mixture into the glue. Stir until it's all mixed together. At first, your mixture will seem like a blob—it's not done yet. Keep stirring! Have kids stir until it has the texture of ricotta cheese.

Pour your blob onto the paper towels and press out the extra water. You've made a polymer that sticks together!

Everyone pair up with your neighbor and tear off a small piece of your polymer. Play with it a bit, stretch it, try to bounce it, and see what it will do. Then stick your polymer onto your neighbor's polymer. David and Jonathan stuck together tightly like your polymers are doing. Good friends should always stick close together!

Lab Results

- **How did David and Jonathan show their friendship and stick together?** (They showed kindness; they kept their promises to each other; etc.)

- **How can we show friendship and stick together with our friends?** Answers will vary.

Super Science Fact

Chemicals that bond together in very long chains are polymers. These chains bend, twist, and get tangled up together. Picture a giant bowl of spaghetti noodles and you'll get a pretty good idea of how polymers act. Because they form long chains, polymers can be flexible but very, very strong and last a long time. That's why it's important to recycle polymers—they won't decompose easily in a landfill.What is the most common polymer you use? Plastic!

Beyond the Laboratory

Truth Explosion: I can be a faithful friend.

For each situation, think of one FAITHFUL response and one UNFAITHFUL response.

1. Your best friend has started eating lunch with someone else.

2. Some of your friends don't want you to hang out with another friend anymore.

3. You think that one of your friends is talking about you behind your back.

What is something you appreciate most in a friend?

What do you think makes you a good friend?

What is one way you can be a better friend?

Hope That Soars

Topic: Hope
Time: 10 minutes
Group Size: Small
Mess Meter: **1** 2 3

Those who hope in the Lord will renew their strength. They will soar on wings like eagles; they will run and not grow weary, they will walk and not be faint.
—2 Corinthians 5:17

Formula for Success

- balloons
- ballpoint pen
- empty and clean 2-liter bottle(s)
- empty and clean peanut butter jar(s)

Oops! Unexpected trouble turns into a lesson on hope that never grows faint.

Truth Explosion: I can be hopeful.

Welcome each of your kids with a balloon. Set out a balloon, a pen and an empty 2-liter bottle for you to use in this experiment.

What things made your week hopeful or "struggle-ful"?

Anyone wish to share a major disappointment?

Today let's talk about hope. Take your ballpoint pen and draw a smiley face on your balloon. Blow it up. **And unexpected troubles!** Release the air from the balloon. **Who's up for a little unexpected trouble?**

Go ahead and prove to me how easy it is to blow up an ordinary balloon. Allow kids to stretch and blow up their balloons.

We're learning today that because God's love is forever, we can be light and hopeful—just like a balloon—even when unexpected things rattle our day. Insert the base of your deflated balloon into the empty 2-liter bottle. Invert the mouthpiece over the bottle opening (see diagram) and blow into the bottle. Blow harder! You will not be able to blow up the balloon completely. **Whew! This is hard. When the pressure builds up there's no telling what'll happen! I think I'm losing hope.** Pass around the extra 2-liter bottles you brought to class. Have your kids take turns inserting their balloons to try and blow them up. **No fainting, please!** After awhile, collect the bottles. **Pressure schmessure! Isaiah 40:31 tells us hope is our gift from God. We will not grow weary in His care. Or faint!** Hold up the peanut butter jar. If your smiley balloon is still useful, hold it up too. **Okay. Let's give this one more try. Let's think. How can I pick up this empty jar with my stretched-out-and-tired-yet-still-hopeful little balloon?** Listen to guesses.

You got it! Place the jar on a table. Hold the deflated balloon inside the jar. Lean over and blow the balloon up. The balloon will quickly fill the insides of

1 Kings 19:1–18; Job 1:1–22; 2:7–10; 42:1–2, 10–13; Acts 16:16–40

the jar. Stand up. The jar will lift off the table. Have kids give it a try with their balloons.

Unexpected things pop up, and we get disappointed or frustrated. But hope surprises us too. Just when things seem impossible, God shows the way with hope that soars on air.

Lab Results

- **What kinds of things do you hope for?** Answers will vary.
- **How does remembering God's care for you help you be hopeful?** (It reminds me that God has taken care of me in the past, and He will take care of me in the future. Everything will be okay because He is in control.)

Super Science Fact

As the air pressure inside the balloon increases so does the air pressure trapped inside the bottle. This balance of pressure and counter-pressure is so strong that no amount of breath can overcome it.

Beyond the Laboratory

Truth Explosion: I can be hopeful.

Complete the following sayings about hope by using words from the word box.

1. Behind every cloud there's a ______________________________.
2. Hope for the _____________ and prepare for the _____________.
3. Hope springs _________________.
4. Look at the ___________________ side.
5. The _________________ hours are just before the dawn.

Word Box

- worst
- eternal
- silver lining
- darkest
- bright
- best

Now use your Bible to complete the following psalms about hope.

1. "You are God my __________________, and my hope is in you all day long" (Psalm 25:5).
2. "Be strong and take ________________ all you who hope in the Lord" (Psalm 31:24).
3. "We wait in hope for the Lord; he is our ___________ and our ___________" (Psalm 33:20).
4. "Yes, my soul, find _________ in God; my hope comes from him" (Psalm 62:5).
5. "I ________ before dawn and cry for ___________; I have put my hope in your word" (Psalm 119:147).

Answers: silver lining, best, worst, eternal, bright, darkest.

That Glazed-Over Look

Topic: God's protection
Time: 15–20 minutes
Group Size: Small groups
Mess Meter: 1 **2** 3

You are my hiding place; you will protect me from trouble and surround me with songs of deliverance.
—Psalm 32:7

Formula for Success

- glazed (or ceramic) flowerpot
- clay (unglazed) flowerpot
- 2 basins of water
- ordinary bathroom scale for weighing them both
- paper
- pencils or pens

Truth Explosion: I can feel safe.

Most kids are eager to forge ahead with new experiences. They sometimes forget how important it is to stay protected from the damaging influences of a culture that does not share their values and beliefs. When your students arrive, have two empty flowerpots on a table in front of them. Split the class in half—one side to represent the clay pot and the other to represent the glazed pot.

We're not planting flowers today. But we are going to figure out the difference between these two pots. They look pretty much the same, don't you think? Just to see what the true similarities and differences are, let's have each group weigh its pot on the scale and record the results on a sheet of paper.

After each side has weighed its pot and recorded the results, place each pot in a basin of water for ten minutes. While you are waiting, ask a few more questions for class discussion.

Address the group with the glazed pot. **What do you think will happen to your pot after it sits in the water for ten minutes? Why do you think so?** Discuss answers.

Psalm 25:21; 2 Thessalonians 3:2–3

Then address the group with the unglazed pot. Ask them the same questions and discuss their answers.

After ten minutes, weigh both pots and compare results.

Lab Results

- **Why do you think the unglazed pot weighed so much more after sitting in the basin of water?** (Without any coating or protection, the water seeped into the clay slowly until it was absorbed.)
- **If water represents the world's bad influences, which kind of pot do you think we should be? Why does God want us to be covered by His protection?** (We should be more like the glazed pot because when the world's bad influences try to seep in, we will be protected against sin.)
- **How do we get "glazed"? Does it happen just by trying to be good?** (God's salvation and the gift of the Holy Spirit protect us. We cannot glaze ourselves, so to speak—it is a gift given to God's children because He loves us and wants us to be holy.)

Super Science Fact

Ceramics are hard, crystalline solids made by heating clay at very high temperatures. Ceramics resist moisture because of a glassy coating that forms from silicon dioxide on its surface. Clay pots have tiny spaces in their structure that absorb and hold water.

Beyond the Laboratory

Truth Explosion: I can feel safe.

1. Do you have a little brother or sister? Imagine that a little toddler was left in a park for an hour totally unprotected. What kind of trouble could he or she get into?

2. Now that you're older, you might not need as much physical protection as you did when you were younger. What kinds of things do your parents still protect you from?

3. What does Psalm 25:21 say is something that can protect us?

4. Take these words from 2 Thessalonians 3:2–3 and figure out the missing blanks by putting the letters in the right order. What is the secret message?

"And **p**ray that we may b**e** delivered from wic**k**ed and evil pe**o**ple, for not everyon**e** ha**s** faith. But the Lord is faithful, **a**nd he will **s**tren**g**then and protect you from the **e**vil one."

_ _ D   _ E _ _ _   M _   _ _ F _!

5. If you have time, paint or print one of today's verses on a ceramic pot to keep in your classroom as a reminder of God's protection.

Answer: God keeps me safe.

Foamy Frenzy

Topic: Purity of heart
Time: 15–20 minutes
Group Size: Individuals
Mess Meter: 1 2 **3**

Formula for Success

- regular-sized bar of Ivory soap*
- paper plate
- microwave
- another bar of soap—a different brand—for comparison *(optional)*

** Only Ivory soap, with its air-filled pockets, creates this interesting effect in the microwave. Don't attempt using another brand.*

A slow-motion explosion can be just as fun as a sudden one—especially when an ordinary object morphs into a new life form! Watch closely as a nuked bar of Ivory soap transforms into a fluffy mass, teaching kids about a clean heart.

Truth Explosion: I can have a pure heart.

When you were little, did you like baths? Some kids love them and some kids hate them. Ask your mom or dad and they might tell you they love a good shower or hot soak in the tub, but a lot of kids run from soap like it's poison. What three-year-old doesn't want to get good and grimy sometimes?

Wash me, and I will be whiter than snow.
—Psalm 51:7

We're going to look at two kinds of soap today—the kind that cleans the outside and the kind that God provides to cleanse our hearts. In order to get a good look at a bar of soap from the inside out, we're going to have to watch a slow-motion eruption. The best way to do this is with a microwave, believe it or not!

Before nuking your soap in the microwave, unwrap both the bar of Ivory soap and another kind, letting kids compare how they both feel and look. Then place your unwrapped bar of Ivory soap on a paper plate. Take your kids to a microwave with a glass window so you can all enjoy the action. Zap the soap for two minutes on full power, and watch the brick transform into a fluffy mass of foam!

This experiment won't harm your microwave, but it can make your kitchen smell like a laundromat for a

few days. And if you want to use your little volcano later, you can actually press together the remaining flakes and use again for washing.

Lab Results

- **Only Ivory soap will work for this experiment. Anybody want to guess why this kind of soap puffs up and others kinds won't?** (Ivory has many more air pockets than other kinds of soap. The air pockets create steam in the microwave, causing it to expand and "explode.")

- **God knows that sometimes our hearts get grimy. Our secret sins, our bad thoughts, our hidden selfishness can fill our hearts with dirt. Simple soap isn't the answer. What does God use to cleanse us?** (God doesn't look at the outside; He looks at the inside. Christ's blood on the cross cleanses us, and God will forgive us if we ask Him.)

- **Let me read 1 John 1:9. "If we confess our sins, he is faithful and just and will forgive us our sins and purify us from all unrighteousness." What does *unrighteousness* mean?** (*Unrighteousness* refers to our sins—the things that keep us from being holy and pure in God's presence.)

Super Science Fact

Unlike other firm soaps, Ivory is made of honeycombed walls filled with tiny air pockets. This is what allows it to float in water and also expand when heated. The pressure of the steam inside the air spaces breaks down the tiny walls inside the soap until the steam has all escaped. Microwaves cause the molecules to vibrate. The faster they vibrate, the hotter it gets.

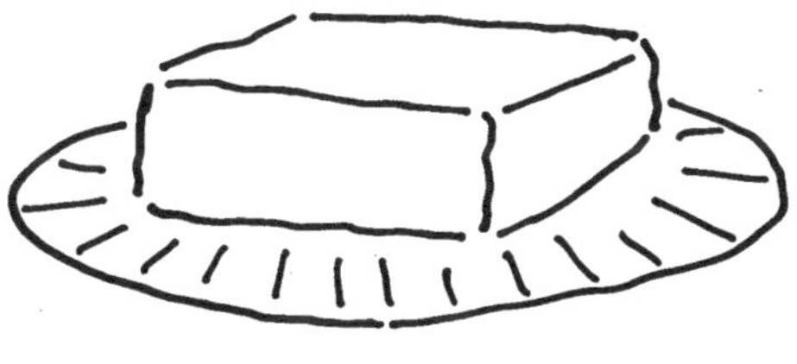

Beyond the Laboratory

Truth Explosion: I can have a pure heart.

You can work with a partner on this discovery mission! Read about the different situations below. You and your partner should try to figure out the best way to keep a pure, clean heart when all the "dirt" around you threatens to leave its stains.

Uh oh ... Stain Alert!	Aaah! ... Sparkling Clean!
A guy in P.E. class flips out when he loses to you in a recreational basketball drill. Now you're his unintentional enemy.	Example: His insecurity is a good excuse to be extra nice—what will getting angry get you? Let him settle down and pick him to be on your team next time.
Last week's blockbuster movie is on everyone's "must see" list—but your folks have said "no way."	
You decided to watch TV last night rather than do that history study guide. Now your teacher wants you to explain. What should you say?	
You told your friend you would watch his tennis match in the finals Friday, but you just got a better offer. He'll understand, right?	

Can You Hear Me Now?

Topic: Prayer
Time: 15–20 minutes
Group Size: Small groups
Mess Meter: **1** 2 3

Speak Lord, for your servant is listening.
—1 Samuel 3:9

Formula for Success

- umbrella
- aluminum foil (have plenty)
- small, hand-held AM/FM radio (This might be tricky to find, but definitely worth it!)
- masking tape
- paper clips *(optional)*

Truth Explosion: I can get tuned to God through prayer.

Prayer is neither a ritual obligation nor some mysterious act of meditation. It is a natural, ongoing conversation between God and His children. Showing kids how radio frequencies operate can help them visualize the importance of "tuning in" to God's voice.

How do you play your favorite music? Do you stream it? Download it? Make a playlist? Well, here's a question for you. When your parents were younger, how do you think they listened to music? Listen to answers. **How about your grandparents?**

Not too long ago, people listened to music primarily through radio waves. Radio waves are constantly in motion in the air, but without the right receiver, those waves will never reach your stereo. We're going to create our own little satellite dish, hoping to figure out where the nearest radio station might be.

Note: You might want to try this on your own first to see how well your homemade satellite picks up the radio frequency in your area.

Have your kids help you line the inside of an umbrella with aluminum foil. Use paperclips along the edges to prevent the foil from slipping off. This will create a makeshift "dish" for your experiment.

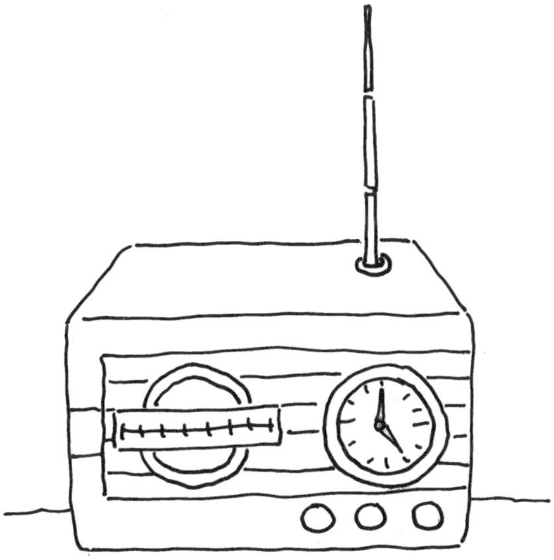

Jeremiah 6:10; Romans 12:12

Turn on a small AM/FM radio and move it along the handle of the umbrella, listening for the position where the station is clearest. You can also try holding the umbrella at different angles. Once you find that perfect spot, tape the radio to the handle. Ta-da! You've created a radio telescope!

Lab Results

- **How can our satellite dish help us figure out the direction of the radio station?** (The point of the umbrella focuses the waves toward the radio receiver. Wherever it's pointing indicates the direction.)
- **What happened when we moved the umbrella at a different angle?** (We lost the correct frequency, making it harder to hear clearly.)
- **In the Old Testament, God spoke to people in a real voice they could hear. How does God speak to us today?** (God uses His Word—the Bible—and the Holy Spirit to instruct us. The Bible says God also makes known His existence through the wonders of nature. Also, when we pray, God can prompt our hearts to obey and know Him better.)
- **So if God is a little like our radio station, what can we do to "tune in" to Him better?** (We can read the Bible, listen to our parents, pray, and obey His commands.)

Super Science Fact

Radio telescopes gather astronomical information on radio frequency radiation. Most radio telescopes are very large and have curved, reflective surfaces, much like the inside of your umbrella. The surface area of a radio telescope concentrates faint radio waves from outer space onto small antennas. The larger the telescope, the more waves it can collect.

Beyond the Laboratory

Truth Explosion: I can get tuned to God through prayer.

1. Just because you have a radio in the house doesn't mean you're listening to it! Read what the prophet Jeremiah said to the city of Jerusalem.

To whom can I speak and give warning?
Who will listen to me?
Their ears are closed so they cannot hear.
The word of the Lord is offensive to them;
they find no pleasure in it.
—Jeremiah 6:10

Wow. Those folks were pretty stubborn. Why do you think some people even today don't want to "tune in" to God?

2. The apostle Paul gave a lot of warnings to people who were just getting to know who Jesus was. Have someone read this passage aloud from Colossians 2:8–10:

"See to it that no one takes you captive through hollow and deceptive philosophy, which depends on human tradition and the elemental spiritual forces of this world rather than on Christ. For in Christ all the fullness of the Deity lives in bodily form, and in Christ you have been brought to fullness. He is the head over every power and authority."

What kind of people does Paul describe in the first part of this passage?

Why is it so cool that we can see God's personality in the real, human person of Jesus?

Why does that make it easier for us to understand God?

Think and Share:
Is it hard for you to talk to God? Why do you think that's true? Share your answer with a friend.

Fabulous Foam!

Topic: Obedience
Time: 15 minutes
Group Size: Individuals
Mess Meter: **1** 2 3

Formula for Success

- 2-liter bottle of clear soda
- glitter (in assorted colors)
- small sequins
- large box of salt with a pourable spout
- small paper cups (3 per child)

Use this activity to help children understand that obeying God is always the best choice.

Truth Explosion: I can obey God.

Before class begins, pour a small amount of sequins and glitter into several separate cups. There should be as many cups with sequins or glitter as there are kids. Also pour a few teaspoons of salt into a cup for each student.

Give each student a cup with glitter or sequins, a cup with salt, and an empty cup.

Love the Lord your God with all your heart and with all your soul and with all your mind.
—Matthew 22:37

Today we're going to do an experiment using soda, salt, and some pretty, sparkly things!

Open the bottle of soda and very slowly fill each empty cup about half full.

Now, very slowly, pour your glitter or sequins into your soda.

Did anything happen to your soda? No! These pretty things didn't make a difference at all! Now let's try some salt. Have kids pour some salt into their cups. A foam fountain will erupt from the cups. When the eruption dies down, students should add a bit more salt to start it again!

If time allows, consider creating a larger fountain by adding the salt to a second, full bottle of soda. It will create a fun, foamy geyser.

What happened this time? The salt made the soda foam! So, all the glitter and sequins we used didn't make a difference, but the salt did. Sometimes things around us can look pretty or fun or exciting (like glitter), but they might not be pleasing to God. He's pleased when we obey Him. What He asks us to do may not always be exciting (like salt), or even something we want to do. But when we obey, some amazing things can happen!

Lab Results

- **Why was it important for Jonah to obey God?** (God cared about the people of Nineveh, God needed Jonah to speak to the people, etc.)

- **How does obeying God show we love Him?** (It shows that we care about what He wants; it shows that we want Him to be in charge; it shows that we want to please Him, etc.)

Super Science Fact

Carbon dioxide gas is pumped into soda. When the bottle is opened, the carbon dioxide molecules rise to the top of the bottle. That's what gives it the fizz! Gases naturally want to expand, and the gas inside the soda is no exception. When you add salt to the soda, thousands of tiny carbon dioxide bubbles form on the surface of each grain of salt. The gas expands and leaves the cups at a very quick rate—taking some of the soda with it.

Beyond the Laboratory

Truth Explosion: I can obey God.

Answer each of the following questions.

1. What are some rules you have to follow at home?

2. What are some rules you have to follow at school?

3. What are some rules your parents have to follow when driving?

4. What are some rules that everyone in society must follow?

5. What are some of God's rules?

6. Why is important to follow rules? Why is it even more important to follow God's rules?

Water Music

Topic: Perseverance
Time: 15 minutes
Group Size: Large group
Mess Meter: **1** 2 3

Do not merely listen to the word, and so deceive yourselves. Do what it says.
—James 1:22

Formula for Success

- 6 to 8 identical drinking glasses
- metal spoons
- pitcher of water
- pony bead, balloon *(optional)*

Truth Explosion: I can do what God asks me to do.

Are you good at listening and doing? It's not enough to know God's Word. We have to "put feet" on what we hear and go out and make it happen. Let's make some music using a simple glass harp. You'll get a turn to play what came before; then chime a note of your own. We'll keep adding notes until we have a wonderful melody.

This will take some perseverance to get right so hang in there!

Fill glasses with varying amounts of water and experiment with different pitches as kids gently tap glasses with spoons. Have students add or empty water from glasses to come up with a pleasing tune.

If you wish, choose a Tune Captain to come up with a melody line. Then assign one glass to one or two students. Tell kids when the Tune Captain taps a certain glass, the students assigned to that glass will perform a corresponding simple action or musical step, such as moving a foot or arm in a certain way. Let the kids make up the actions that will go with each glass. Practice makes permanent! Then have the Tune Captain play the tune slowly while the class displays their steps in sequence. Quicken the pace for added fun!

Genesis 37:1–36; Ezra 7; Nehemiah 6–8; Matthew 1:18—2:15

Lab Results

- **There's more to music than just listening. Sometimes you need to move your feet and tap to the beat! Why does God want us to share His love with others instead of keeping it all to ourselves?** (Because He wants all people to know and love Him, because He uses us to accomplish His plans in the world)

- **How can you "do what the Word says" this week?** Answers will vary.

- **When can you make a glass harp at home and play it with your family?** Answers will vary.

We can put God's Word into action when we rely on His strength. Whatever the circumstances, discouragement or opposition, play on! And spread the Word of God.

Super Science Fact

Hitting the glass causes it to vibrate. High and low sounds "vibrate" to produce sound. The volume of water in the glass will determine the speed of the vibration—and thus the pitch. The more water in the glass, the slower the vibrations and the deeper the tone.

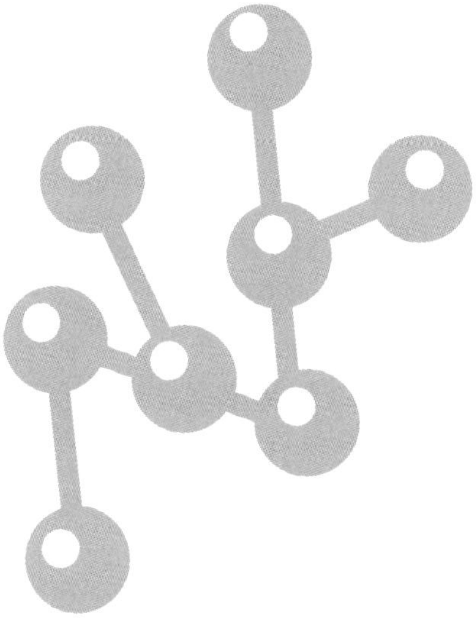

Beyond the Laboratory

Truth Explosion: I can do what God asks me to do.

Read the following statements. Underline the things you are able to do.

I can tie my shoes.
I can count to 20 in Spanish.
I can say the alphabet backwards.
I can drive a car.
I can groom a dog.
I can fly an airplane.
I can stand on my head.
I can ride a bike.
I can skate.

Now think of some of the things God would like you to do. List three in the spaces below.

1.

2.

3.

Draw a star beside the one that you will do first. Ask God to help you, and then go for it!

My Beautiful Balloon

Topic: Faith
Time: 5–10 minutes
Group Size: Individual or pairs
Mess Meter: 1 **2** 3

Now faith is confidence in what we hope for and assurance about what we do not see.
—Hebrews 11:1

Formula for Success

- balloons
- empty and clean soda bottle (or juice bottle)
- water
- baking soda
- the juice from one lemon
- straw
- colorful metallic confetti, penny *(optional)*

Up, up, and away! Use this experiment to see how an invisible faith in God grows and grows.

Truth Explosion: I can make choices that honor God.

For a quick warm-up to this activity, start with a simple experiment on static electricity. Open the packet of tabletop confetti and pour a little of it into a clean and dry soda bottle. Now stretch your balloon and place it over the mouth of the bottle. Turn the bottle over and shake the confetti into the balloon. Blow up the balloon, knot, and rub it against a student's hair. Static electricity will cause the confetti to jump and stick to the sides of the balloon! (Fun Science Fact: If two objects attract and stick together, they have opposite charges.) **Let's do another experiment that will help us remember that God is everywhere—even if we can't see Him. Allow God's supernatural powers to help invisible faith grow in you!**

Fill the bottle with one-fourth cup of water.

How do worries and fears keep us from growing in faith? Does Jesus understand this about day-to-day worries?

Sprinkle one teaspoon of baking soda into the bottle and stir with the straw. Pour in the lemon juice. Quickly stretch an un-inflated balloon and place it over the mouth of the bottle.

We don't "see" anything inside the bottle, do we? But we have faith that there's something in there. Let's prove it!

Watch as the balloon inflates—and the confetti twinkles and shines when held close to a light source!

Our experiment is a fun way to remember that although we don't see faith, we can trust its power to connect to God.

Matthew 8:5–13; Mark 10:46–52; Luke 8:4–8, 11–15

Lab Results

- **We can't see the gas, but we know that it's in there. How does this remind you of many of Jesus' miracles?** (I never saw them, but I believe they are true. Jesus' followers couldn't see His power, but they trusted that it was real and that Jesus' power came from God.)

- **What "earthly" things crowd out God and leave little room for His power to work miracles in our lives?** (busy schedules, preoccupation with things, anger, etc.)

- **Can you think of something you might have to give up to allow faith to grow in you?** Answers will vary.

Super Science Fact

When a base (baking soda) and an acid (lemon juice) come together the resulting reaction forms a clear, colorless gas known as carbon dioxide. As the gas rises it fills the empty balloon.

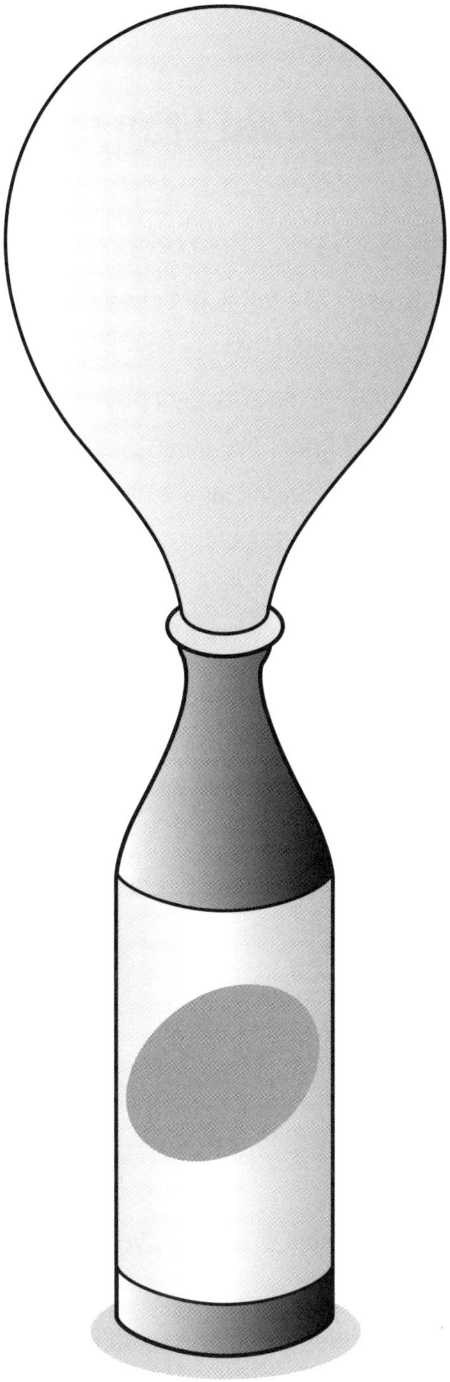

Beyond the Laboratory

Truth Explosion: I can make choices that honor God.

Read through the following choices and circle the one you would choose.

1. Would you rather eat spinach or tacos?
2. Would you rather play ping pong or soccer?
3. Would you rather live on an island or a mountain?
4. Would you rather wear a mohawk or a cowboy hat?
5. Would you rather eat chocolate or cotton candy?
6. Would you rather ride a bike or a skateboard?
7. Would you rather have fur or feathers?
8. Would you rather get a cat or a dog?
9. Would you rather play in the sand or in the snow?
10. Would you rather read a book or watch a movie?

Now think of a really tough choice you are facing right now.

Why is it so difficult?

How does it make you feel?

What do you want to do?

What do you think God wants you to do?

What about this choice makes you afraid?

Take a few moments and say a prayer, asking God to help you make the right choice.

Can't Pop My Joy

Topic: Joy
Time: 10–20 minutes
Group Size: Individual
Mess Meter: **1** 2 3

The Lord is my strength and my shield; my heart trusts in him, and he helps me. My heart leaps for joy, and with my song I praise him.
—Psalm 28:7

Formula for Success

- light-colored 10-inch balloons
- large paper bag
- sewing needle
- small and large balloons *(optional)*

Find the inner joy of knowing Jesus.

Truth Explosion: I can worship Jesus as my Savior.

Before class, stretch out two light-colored balloons. Use the rubber end of a pencil to push one balloon inside the other, leaving the lip of the internal balloon extended. Fully blow up the outer balloon. Pinch the ends and hold the balloons up to the light. You should see the inner balloon resting limply inside the other. Finally, blow up the inner balloon half as full as the outer one. You'll need lip and cheek muscles to push the air through! One knot will close both balloons. Blow up two or three balloon-in-balloon pairs and drop them inside a bag.

When you're ready to begin class, grab the bag of balloons and place it close to you. Don't forget to thread a sewing needle into your sleeve cuff. Pass out new balloons to your kids. Ask students to blow them up and pinch them shut with their fingers. Do not knot. Make sure to blow up a balloon for yourself.

What kind of feelings could balloons represent?

We might say that balloons represent the way we feel when we have no joy or excitement in our hearts. We feel deflated as if the air swooshed right out of us. Release your balloon and let kids to do the same. Watch as balloons zip through the room and fall.

Take a "balloon-within-a-balloon" from the bag by your side and hold it high for kids to see. **Here's another balloon, and it represents something completely different. Joy! A joy so strong, nothing can pop it!** Remove the needle from your sleeve and prick the top of the outer balloon. Pop! Still, your kids will be surprised to see the fully intact balloon inside! Use your extra balloons if the trick doesn't work the first time.

Luke 2:1–20; John 3:1–21; 20:1–18

Joy is knowing that all year long the Son of God lives inside of you. No matter what happens on the outside, you can have joy on the inside. If you have time and supplies let kids prepare their own double balloons and practice popping the outer one.

We might think a lot of things make us happy at least for the moment. But true joy can bubble up even when we're having hard times. Recognize the joy that comes from Jesus living inside you!

Something Extra!

This experiment can be done in reverse, but it's a lot trickier. Grab a small and a large balloon. Follow the instructions above but knot the smaller, internal balloon and push it inside the larger balloon. The inner balloon should float freely inside. Then blow up the larger balloon half full. Squeeze the smaller balloon against the knotted part of the outer balloon. Press your needle into the side of the outer balloon, where the balloons touch, just enough to leave an indentation. Pop! The inner balloon should pop, leaving the outer balloon intact.

Lab Results

- **Show me with your face what you feel like on the inside when you're joyful.**
- **How do we show our joy when we worship?** (We sing and praise God; we shout to God; we clap our hands, etc.)
- **How is joy different from happiness?** (Happiness is based on what is taking place in our lives. Joy exists no matter what is going on around us.)

Super Science Fact

The amount of air in a filled balloon determines the flexibility of its skin and its ability to withstand pressure. A hole or break in the balloon's skin is a point of weakness, which causes a rapid tear and, thus, an overall surface failure.

Beyond the Laboratory

Truth Explosion: I can worship Jesus as my Savior.

Match each of the following names for Jesus with the correct Scripture verse.

1. Deliverer	a. Revelation 22:13
2. Good Shepherd	b. Job 19:25
3. Messiah	c. John 6:35
4. Redeemer	d. Matthew 3:17
5. Son of God	e. Romans 11:26
6. King of Kings	f. John 1:41
7. Bread of Life	g. 1 Corinthians 10:4
8. Lamb	h. John 10:11
9. Rock	i. Revelation 17:14
10. Alpha and Omega	j. John 1:29

Take a few moments and think about who Jesus is to you. Write a few words or phrases that describe Him in the space below. Then say a prayer of praise, thanking God for Jesus and all He means to you.

Answers: e, h, f, b, d, i, c, j, g, a.

Pounding Palms

Topic: Praise
Time: 15–20 minutes
Group Size: Individual
Mess Meter: 1 **2** 3

Formula for Success

- boards, approximately 8" x 10" (1 per child)
- pushpins (4 per child)
- palm leaves (1 per child; check with your local florist)
- muslin fabric, cut in pieces about 1" smaller than the boards (1 piece per child)
- hammers or mallets (1 per child)

The crowd's cheers turned quickly to shouts of anger when they realized He wasn't the king they expected. But we can joyfully praise Him as our unchanging King and Savior forever!

Truth Explosion: I can joyfully praise Jesus!

This activity can get a little loud. Try to find an area where you won't disturb a neighboring class, or go outside. Better yet, kids of all ages (including the grown-up kind) can enjoy this activity—so do it together!

Jesus Christ is the same yesterday and today and forever.
—Hebrews 13:8

If you don't have a saw, don't worry. Many home improvement stores will cut the boards for you. They don't have to be a uniform size—scrap pieces will work well too. Cut boards and muslin before class.

Introduce the activity by talking about chlorophyll. Give each student a palm leaf. **Does anyone know what makes our palm leaves green? It's chlorophyll!** Have children repeat the word *chlorophyll* a few times. **Chlorophyll is a cool chemical hidden inside plants that lets them make their own food. Let's use the chlorophyll in our palm leaves to make a cool leaf print!**

Place the palm leaves on the boards. Have each child cover a palm leaf with a piece of muslin.

Have children tack the muslin in place at the corners with pushpins. Adults may need to help with this part.

Have children lightly pound the muslin with hammers until the print of the leaf shows through on the cloth. Remind children to keep their fingers away from the hammers!

Allow children to take home the completed prints.

Lab Results

- **Why did people place palm leaves in front of Jesus?** (to welcome Him, to praise Him, to show He is special)
- **What are some ways we can praise Jesus as our King?** (singing, dancing, clapping, raising our hands)
- **How does it make you feel to know Jesus never changes?** (safe, happy, thankful, relieved)

Super Science Fact

Plant cells, called chloroplasts, are filled with a green chemical called chlorophyll. Chlorophyll is required for photosynthesis—the process in which plants convert sunlight into nutrients. In this activity, the chloroplasts are broken as the leaves are hammered. Their chlorophyll is released onto the fabric, turning it green.

Beyond the Laboratory

Truth Explosion: I can joyfully praise Jesus!

"**Shout for joy** to the LORD, all the earth. Worship the LORD with gladness;
come before him with joyful songs."
—Psalm 100:1–2

"Therefore, since we are receiving a kingdom that cannot be shaken,
let us be **thankful, and so worship God** acceptably with reverence and awe."
—Hebrews 12:28

"Let the message of Christ dwell among you richly as you teach and admonish one another with all wisdom through psalms, hymns, and songs from the Spirit, **singing to God with gratitude in your hearts.** And whatever you do, whether in word or deed, do it all in the name of the Lord Jesus, **giving thanks** to God the Father through him."
—Colossians 3:16–17

"**Rejoice always, pray** continually, **give thanks in all circumstances**;
for this is God's will for you in Christ Jesus."
—1 Thessalonians 5:16–18

In the space below, write a joyful letter of praise to Jesus.

Stuffed on Prayer

Topic: Prayer
Time: 10 minutes
Group Size: Pairs or small groups
Mess Meter: 1 **2** 3

Do not be anxious about anything, but in every situation, by prayer and petition, with thanksgiving, present your requests to God.
—Philippians 4:6

Formula for Success

- paper
- clear drinking cups
- shallow basin
- water

Use the natural curiosity found in children to help them learn to pray with confidence.

Truth Explosion: I can pray with confidence.

Depending on the size of your group, you may want to have kids try this activity in pairs or small groups. Demonstrate first; then let kids try.

Our Truth Explosion tells us that because God listens, we can pray with confidence. Pour an inch of water into the basin. Hold up the newspaper. **I feel confident I can place this newspaper in the water and it will not get wet!**

Stuff a rolled up wad of paper tightly into the jar so it won't fall out. Then set the jar (open end down) into the basin of water. If you lift the jar straight out, the newspaper will stay nice and dry.

Air is lighter than water. You can't see it, but you know it's there. It's what kept the water from the newspaper. In the same way, we can't see God, but when we pray, His presence surrounds us. We can pray confidently because God listens.

Encourage kids to take turns trying this experiment in their small groups.

God is listening. We can talk to Him about anything, anytime, anywhere. He cares about you!

1 Kings 18:18–45; Daniel 6:1–28; Luke 11:1–4; Acts 12:1–17

Lab Results

- **Name two tasks you can perform more confidently when you ask God to help you.** Answers will vary.
- **How can God's presence surrounding you help you head off temptation to do something you know is wrong?** (Knowing God is with me can help me be brave enough to make a hard decision. It can remind me to think of what God wants and not what I want.)
- **What is your favorite time of day to pray?** Answers will vary.

Super Science Fact

Air is invisible. Yet it is made up of tiny particles that take up space. In today's experiment, the air blocks the water from entering the glass. But … if you could push your glass deep enough (into a lake, pond, or ocean) the water pressure would eventually allow water to seep into the glass and wet the newspaper.

Beyond the Laboratory

Truth Explosion: I can pray with confidence.

The Bible is filled with examples of people who boldly approached Jesus, confident He could give them what they needed. Check out the examples below and write a few words summarizing each passage. Then write about an example from your life, telling how you felt and what happened.

Luke 7:1–10

Mark 2:1–12

Luke 17:11–17

Mathew 9:18–26

Luke 7:37–50

My example:

"Therefore I tell you, whatever you ask for in prayer, believe that you have received it, and it will be yours."
Mark 11:24

Wet Rocks

Topic: Confidence
Time: 15 minutes
Group Size: Individuals or pairs
Mess Meter: 1 **2** 3

Yes, my soul, find rest in God;
my hope comes from him.
—Psalm 62:5

Formula for Success

- plastic cups
- a cup of water
- tissues
- rubber bands
- small stones (or marbles)

It's not rocket science! Let Jesus encourage your kids' faith and give them the confidence to believe He is the Son of God.

Truth Explosion: I can believe in Jesus.

Do friends joke or brag they can do amazing, super-human things that no one else can do? Like X-ray vision or mind control? Is your response a firm, "Yeah, right!" Let's do an experiment to see, firsthand, the heavy weight doubt puts on our spiritual lives.

Place the empty cups on the table and the cup of water nearby. Have one of your students lay a tissue over the empty cup and gently secure it with a rubber band. Ask another student to dip his or her fingers into the glass of water and drop four or five water droplets onto the tissue. Then have the class gather.

Doubts can lead us away from Jesus. Allow kids to express when doubt has taken them away from Jesus' wisdom and promise for their lives. With each response have students lightly place one stone at a time on the wet tissue. Be listening for confusion between questions and doubts. It's healthy to ask questions so we can have stronger faith.

The big question is this: how long before the faithful tissue breaks under the weight of doubt? Depending on the strength of the tissue, it will hold 7 to 12 small stones before splitting. Two layered tissues will hold twice as many stones—or more.

Even Jesus' friends and followers struggled with doubt. When Jesus appeared to the disciples after His resurrection, Thomas wanted proof it was really Him. Like the disciples, we have a choice. We can put our faith and hope in Jesus, or we can stand still and break under the pressure of doubt. Make your choice a confident first step toward Jesus!

Jesus celebrated people who would put their faith in Him long after His death. He made it a point to call these believers blessed (John 20:29)**! Because Jesus helps us with doubts, we can believe in Him.**

Luke 2:41–52; John 19:1–18; 20:1–8, 19–31; Acts 16:16–40

Lab Results

- **What kinds of pressures and pains cause people to doubt their faith in Jesus?** (getting bullied, death or illness, parent's job loss, divorce, moving to a new school, losing friends, and so on)

- **In an ordinary day, when does doubt weigh heavy on your mind?** Answers will vary.

- **When is it easiest to believe Jesus is really with you? Why?** (Possible answers: When things are going well, because I know the blessings are from Him. When things are hard, because I know He gives me strength to get through the hard times.)

Beyond the Laboratory

Truth Explosion: I can believe in Jesus.

Look at this list. Circle the people and things you believe in.

fairy godmothers	**fear**
dinosaurs	**sea horses**
oxygen	**freedom**
Bigfoot	**George Washington**
gravity	**the equator**

Look at the things you've circled. Now draw a star next to the ones that you've actually seen for yourself. Write the total number here: ________

Why do you believe in things you've never seen? Is it easier to believe in something you can't see or something you can see? Why?

Read Mark 9:17–24. Write the words the boy's father said in verse 24:

____

Think of a situation in your life in which you're struggling to believe in God's power and control. Use the written words above as a prayer, asking God to increase your belief and trust in Him.

Marshmallow Madness

Topic: Transformation
Time: 15–20 minutes
Group Size: Small groups
Mess Meter: 1 **2** 3

Therefore, if anyone is in Christ, the new creation has come: The old has gone, the new is here!
—1 Corinthians 5:17

Formula for Success

- marshmallows
- paper plate
- microwave

Is it possible to toast only the inside of a marshmallow? Kids can check out a surprising truth about microwave cooking while they discover that God transforms us from the inside out.

Truth Explosion: I can let Jesus change me from the inside out.

Roasting marshmallows is easy, right? Grab a stick and a roaring campfire, and you've got yourself a toasty, golden glob of summertime memories. But like our own spiritual condition, what if we could change the inside of a marshmallow first? As your kids gather around a microwave window, not only will they enjoy the visual show, but they will also explore the paradox of God's inside-out transformation.

How many of you have roasted marshmallows over a campfire? Have you ever noticed that everyone has a different cooking method? Some like to slowly rotate the stick at a perfect distance from the flame and others torch the poor puffball until it looks like a melted hockey puck. What's your method? Listen as kids share their stories.

We're going to have to sneak a peek at our experiment today through a window because it will take place in a microwave. Let's see what happens when we nuke this poor fellow on high.

Put a marshmallow on a paper plate and cook it on high in the microwave for about a minute and a half. Those mysterious microwaves will begin to transform that little puff, almost making it seem like a living creature. It will grow up to three times its original size, quivering and swaying as it

Proverbs 20:27; Romans 12:2; 2 Corinthians 3:18

cooks. Once the puffing has stopped, turn off your microwave; otherwise, the entire marshmallow will cook and you'll have quite a mess to clean up!

When you remove the marshmallow, don't touch it—it's very hot! While it cools for several minutes, it will begin to shrink and shrivel. The outside will look white and chalky—almost uncooked. But when your group breaks it open, the inside will be brown! You've actually "toasted" your marshmallow from the inside out!

Lab Results

- **What do you think caused only the inside of the marshmallow to cook?** (The microwave targeted the water, fats, and sugars deep inside. The outside surface was kept cooler by the escaping steam, but the inside turned brown from the intense heat.)
- **How is this different from how a campfire cooks a marshmallow?** (A fire cooks the outside surface first, so the surface gets brown before anything else.)
- **Like the microwave, God wants to change the inside of us first. How does He do that?** (God forgives us of our sins when we ask Him. He looks at our motives, our hearts and our deepest secrets rather than looking at what others see on the outside.)

Super Science Fact

Microwaves cook food by vibrating the water, fat, and other molecules inside of food. The faster the molecules vibrate, the hotter the food gets. Sugar browns when it is cooked at high temperatures.

Beyond the Laboratory

Truth Explosion: I can let Jesus change me from the inside out.

"Do not conform to the pattern of this world, but be transformed by the renewing of your mind. Then you will be able to test and approve what God's will is—his good, pleasing and perfect will."
—Romans 12:2

"The human spirit is the lamp of the Lord that sheds light on one's inmost being."
—Proverbs 20:27

"And we all, who with unveiled faces contemplate the Lord's glory, are being transformed into his image with ever-increasing glory, which comes from the Lord, who is the Spirit."
—2 Corinthians 3:18

What do these three verses have in common? Write down some ideas.

We can change the outside by ourselves, but we need God to change the inside. Why is the inside even more important?

What makes a lamp such a good metaphor in the second verse? What else would be a good comparison for God's searching eyes?

Writing to Explore: Choose one of the following "secret" places and imagine it to be a symbol for your inner life—your thoughts, dreams, and secrets. If we were an explorer, archeologist, or hunter, what might we find there? Write a creative paragraph on a separate piece of paper.

Here is an idea starter: Far away in the corner of a castle sits a hidden room full of my worst thoughts. From the outside you can't see it, but behind a locked door lies a room that hasn't been cleaned in years …

- a cave
- the deepest part of the ocean
- a treasure chest
- a secret chamber
- a maze
- a hidden room in a castle
- a mountain crevice
- another planet

A Funnel of Fun!

Topic: Integrity
Time: 5 minutes
Group Size: Individuals or pairs
Mess Meter: **1** 2 3

The fruit of the Spirit is love, joy, peace, forbearance, kindness, goodness, faithfulness, gentleness and self-control.
—Galatians 5:22–23

Formula for Success

- clean household funnels
- table tennis balls

With a huff and a puff, kids find out they need God's strength to make choices that please Him.

Truth Explosion: I can follow Jesus' teachings.

With His help, God wants us to produce the fruit of the Spirit. Unfortunately, experience teaches us that our human nature prefers its own sinful way.

Did you feel really selfish this week? Accept responses. **Did you feel like quitting something hard?**

We can agree that on our own it's an impossible task to attain the joy, love, and faithfulness God wants us to have. Still we try and try to go it alone!

Hold out the funnel and the table tennis ball. **What would you think if I told you I'm known far and wide for having a pair of mighty lungs? I can take a really deep breath and blow harder than anyone you know. Suppose I said I could blow this little ball up to the ceiling?**

Drop the ball into the funnel. Tilt your head back and put the funnel's narrow end near your lips. **How long will it be before I blow the ball inside this funnel up to the ceiling?**

Have your kids shout out guesses. Then blow! The harder you blow the higher the ball will go—but it will not hit the ceiling. The ball will simply remain suspended in the air a short distance away from the funnel. **I'm trying! I'm trying!** Take a deep breath and try again.

Note: The only way to get the ball out of the funnel is to blow across the top of the funnel! If you have extra funnels and balls, give kids a chance to try.

I admit it. I can't do it! I hope we've all learned that we can't overcome our own selfish ways using just our strength.

Our actions and behaviors alone do not allow us to live the kind of joyful, unselfish lives God has planned for us, try and try as we might. Only with the Holy Spirit can we demonstrate the behavior and attitude needed to produce His fruit.

Lab Results

- **Can anyone tell about a time when God helped you conquer a selfish, mean, or discouraging feeling?** Answers will vary.
- **Why is trying on your own to be joyful or patient not enough to make it happen?** (because my strength is not enough; I get discouraged or angry; and so on)
- **Tell about a time when God's Spirit helped you be loving, joyful, or patient.** Answers will vary.

Super Science Fact

Bernoulli's Principle states that the rapid moving air in a funnel results in a decrease in air pressure. This causes the ball to be pushed into the funnel by the higher air pressure sitting on top. A funnel attached to a constant blowing air supply can be held upside down and the ball will not fly out!

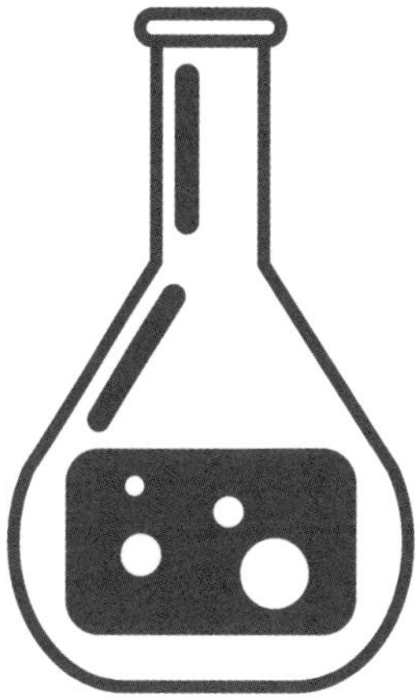

Beyond the Laboratory

Truth Explosion: I can follow Jesus' teachings.

The teachings of Jesus all come down to love. Matthew 22:35–40 says:

"Hearing that Jesus had silenced the Sadducees, the Pharisees got together. One of them, an expert in the law, tested him with this question: 'Teacher, which is the greatest commandment in the Law?' Jesus replied: 'Love the Lord your God with all your heart and with all your soul and with all your mind.' This is the first and greatest commandment. And the second is like it: 'Love your neighbor as yourself.' All the Law and the Prophets hang on these two commandments."

Is love your first response to most situations? Why or why not?

Read the examples below and discuss with a friend how a loving response could make a difference in each situation:

Your little sister breaks accidentally breaks your phone.

Your dad just lost his job.

Your best friend's parents are getting divorced.

You got cut from your soccer team.

Your brother blamed you for something you didn't do.

Ask God to help you follow the teachings of Jesus and respond with love. Every. Single. Time.

There's Gold in Them Thar Hills!

Topic: Treasure, God's kingdom
Time: 15–20 minutes
Group Size: Small groups
Mess Meter: 1 2 **3**

But store up for yourselves treasures in heaven, where moths and vermin do not destroy, and where thieves do not break in and steal. For where your treasure is, there your heart will be also.
—Matthew 6:20–21

Formula for Success

- aluminum pie pans
- sand
- a collection of costume jewelry
- water
- paper towels
- bowls

Does God ever sift out the worthless matter from our lives? During this experiment, kids discover that the most precious materials won't be washed away.

Truth Explosion: I can search for the treasures of God's kingdom.

Before you start, mix dry sand or dirt with some costume jewelry in a tray or aluminum pie pan for each group of students. This is dirt-time. Needless to say, leave those expensive heirlooms back home in the jewelry chest! You can even use metal bolts or coins if you can't find enough pieces of costume jewelry.

Living here on Earth, it's sometimes hard to see which things are really valuable and which things just wash away. Jesus sometimes compares really important things—like wisdom and truth—to treasures that we must diligently search for. We're going to see what happens when we try to separate the important things from the worthless things.

Present a sand-and-treasure tray to each group of students. Tell them they have to figure out a way to separate the sand from the larger pieces without using magnets or simply picking them out. They can use water, a bowl, paper towels or other common objects in the classroom. Since this age group loves competition, you could even set a timer, or give first place to the group that solves the problem first.

Proverbs 2:1–5; Colossians 2:2–3

Most groups will figure out that by adding water to the pan and slowly pouring it out, the smaller particles will combine with the water and float away, leaving behind the "precious jewels." Other groups might decide to punch medium-sized holes in the bottom of the pan to let the sand and water escape.

Lab Results

- **This experiment is a little like the gold panning that the early Californians did in the 1800s. How is searching for God's treasures a lot like panning for precious metals?** (We are trying to reveal the things that have real value, such as wisdom or truth.)

- **Sometimes the Gold Rush participants found "fool's gold"—a fake material that looked a lot like gold but was really something called pyrite. What are some examples of the world's "fool's gold" that might lure people into believing it has value when it really doesn't?** (Sometimes people think that money, fancy possessions or even popularity is the most valuable thing on Earth. But it won't last like the eternal treasures of God.)

- **What did you have to do before the sand and jewelry separated? How does God sometimes get us to see the lasting treasures He wants to give us?** (Seeing God's treasures sometimes requires some effort on our part. We might have to "shake up" our lives through study and effort in order to expose the truths of the Bible.)

Super Science Fact

Miners used the technique of panning to separate gold from sand and dirt by using the principles of density. When water swirled around the pan, the heavier materials sank to the bottom while the rest was washed away. Gold nuggets are made of pure gold. A rock that has a mixture of useful metals like gold or iron and worthless materials is called an ore.

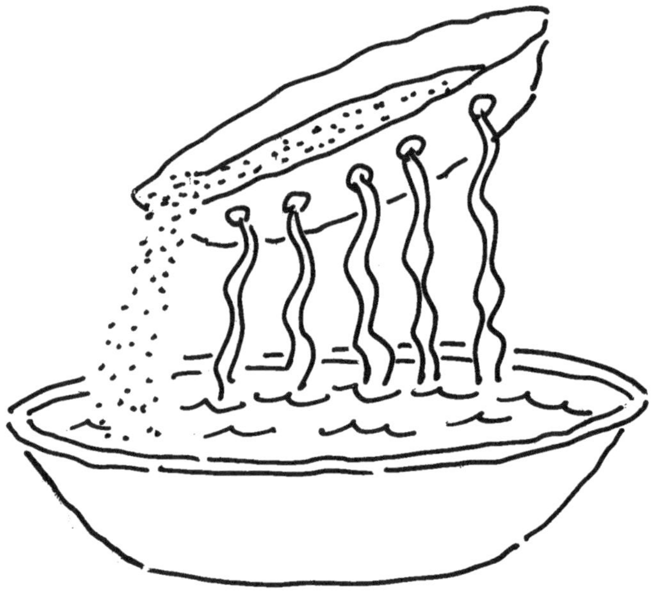

Beyond the Laboratory

Truth Explosion: I can search for the treasures of God's kingdom.

1. If you were a miner searching for diamonds or emeralds or opals deep within Earth, what equipment would you need to get started?

2. We live in God's kingdom here and now. There are wonderful treasures to be discovered in God's kingdom. Skim Matthew 3–24, and jot down the treasures you unearth.

3. Find Psalm 119:127 in your Bible and read it out loud to a partner. Then let your partner read it back to you.

Why are God's commands even better than gold?

In the 1850s, some gold panners ended up killing each other over the rights to the gold they had discovered. Why does gold make some people so greedy?

Can you ever have too much of God?

4. Use your Bible to fill in the missing words in the blanks below.

"My son, if you accept my words
and store up my __________within you,
turning your ear to __________
and applying your ________to understanding—
indeed, if you call out for insight
and cry aloud for understanding,
and if you look for it as for ________
and search for it as for _________treasure,
then you will understand the ______of the ________
and find the _____________ of God."
—Proverbs 2:1–5

What a Mess! The Truth about Sticky Situations

Topic: Attitudes
Time: 15–20 minutes
Group Size: Small groups
Mess Meter: 1 **2** 3

Formula for Success

- skim milk
- baking soda
- vinegar
- coffee filter
- plastic spoon
- 2 plastic cups
- paper plate

When you add a sour attitude to your day, you'll end up stuck!

Truth Explosion: I can have an attitude of gratitude.

This experiment allows you to demonstrate a chemical reaction that changes ordinary ingredients into homemade, natural glue.

A sour attitude has ruined many a sweet day. Agreed? What's your story? Wait for answers. **We can't always help what happens to us, whether it's rain on the day of the championship game or a disappointing turn-out for your summertime lemonade business. Bad news, right? Let's see this principle played out with a little crazy science. What might happen when we add a sour attitude to an otherwise sweet day?**

Give thanks to the Lord, for he is good;
his love endures forever.
—Psalm 106:1

Pour about one-half cup of skim milk into a plastic cup. Add two tablespoons of vinegar and stir to mix.

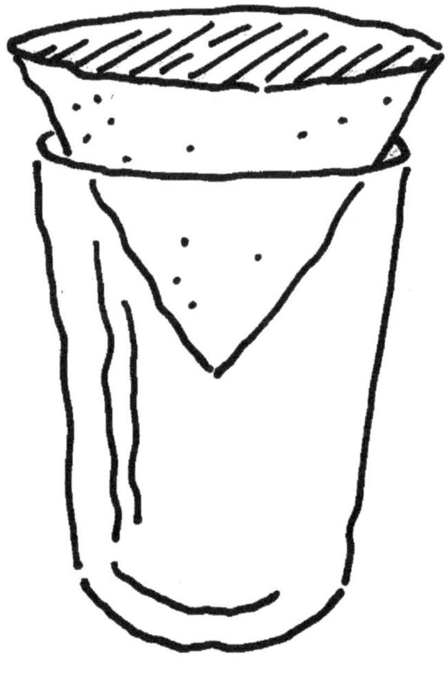

Let one of your students pour the mixture through a coffee filter resting over another cup.

Use a plastic spoon to scrape off the solid material that collects on the filter. Place this thicker material onto a paper plate. Add a pea-sized amount of baking soda to the mixture and stir. You've made a natural glue! Let students try gluing two pieces of paper together to see how well the glue works.

Lab Results

- **Our experiment shows what happens to one material when another one is added. How can our attitude make a "chemical change" in our day?** (A bad attitude can sour an otherwise good situation, like when our teacher buys us a treat, but we complain instead of being thankful. Likewise, a good attitude can turn something around for the better. For example, maybe we didn't win a game, but we were able to have fun with our teammates anyway.)
- **We've all ruined something good because we grumbled and complained. Give me an example.** Answers will vary.
- **Did it take much vinegar to make the milk goopy? What does this tell us about a bad attitude?** (A little bit of negativity can have a big impact on others.)

Super Science Fact

Chemical reaction is another name for a chemical change. During this kind of chemical reaction, two or more substances combine to make a new substance. You can make a chemical reaction happen faster or slower. One way to do this is by physical manipulation—such as stirring.

Beyond the Laboratory

Truth Explosion: I can have an attitude of gratitude.

1. Have you ever tasted a little bit of vinegar by itself? Ask your teacher if you can dip your finger in it and have a taste. How is vinegar a little bit like a negative attitude?

2. Have you ever heard people use the phrase "God's will"? This phrase refers not only to the things God is going to do without anyone's help, but also the instructions in the Bible he wants us to practice. Look up 1 Thessalonians 5:18.

What does this verse say is "God's will" for you?

What kind of situation would make it very hard for you to be thankful?

3. Turn to a friend and ask him or her to fill in the blank: I would find it very disappointing this week if ______________________ happened. Now ask your friend to tell you how he or she could turn that bad situation into something good with the right, thankful attitude.

4. Everyone in your class can read the following verse together out loud:

"Let the word of Christ dwell among you richly as you teach and admonish one another with all wisdom through psalms, hymns, and songs from the Spirit, singing to God with gratitude in your hearts."
—Colossians 3:16

5. One the lines below write three high-energy words from the verse above:

____________________ _________________________ ____________________

Why did you pick these three? What special meaning do they hold for you?

Splat! The Sky Is Falling!

Topic: Staying close to God
Time: 15–20 minutes
Group Size: Small groups
Mess Meter: 1 **2** 3

But as for me, it is good to be near God. I have made the Sovereign Lord my refuge; I will tell of all your deeds.
—Psalm 73:28

Formula for Success

- large sandbox (or plastic tub)
- sand (or soft dirt)
- ladder
- variety of round weights from small to large, such as marbles, a round paper weight, even a bowling ball!

The further away from God we go, the harder we fall. By measuring the effect of craters on Earth's surface, kids begin to see how a big fall changes everything.

Truth Explosion: I can stick close to God.

Craters. Golf divots. Gouges in the kitchen floor. With the right force, anything can create an impression on everyday surfaces. During this drop-and-watch activity, your kids can discover the effect of distance and force on a non-solid surface. Besides being a lot of fun (who doesn't like to drop things and watch what happens?), this experiment will teach kids that drifting away from God is never a good idea.

Note: Since your group will be dropping things from different heights, be careful to keep students away from the tub of sand to avoid injury. When someone climbs the ladder, always have a spotter stand below to stabilize the climb.

Several years ago, a TV show featured the host dropping things off of the roof of a building. Does that sound like fun to you? Who hasn't been tempted, while looking down over a high ledge, to drop stuff down below—just to see what happens? Feel free to share silly stories. **Our experiment today requires us to be careful, so you don't want to do this on your own without an adult to help you.**

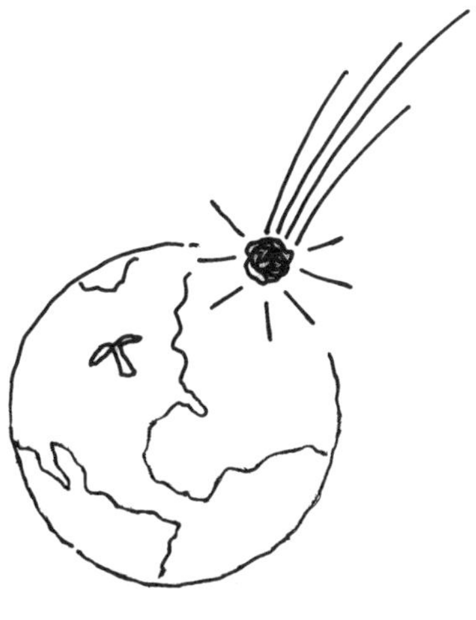

Hebrews 10:22; James 4:8

Let's drop some items into a large sandbox and see what happens. What do you think will happen when we are farther away from the sand? What about when we're closer? What do you think will happen with lighter objects? Heavier objects?

You will probably want to do this experiment outdoors. Start with smaller items, such as a marble or a small paperweight. Drop these objects into the sand from different heights, letting kids use the ladder as appropriate.

Observe the craters left behind after you've carefully removed the objects. You can assign "sand smoothers" to smooth out the surface of the sand after each drop. Culminate with a carefully-dropped bowling ball or other round, heavy weight. You can record your findings with a simple chart like the one on the next page.

Lab Results

- **Besides the weight of the object, what else determined the mess we made in the sandbox?** (The height of the object when it was released affected the crater.)
- **We are all going to drift away from God at times. What happens if we've drifted far away from God and then we "fall"?** (When we finally "fall," it's going to hurt more and cause more damage in the end.)
- **What kind of damage can be created when we move away from God?** Answers will vary. Some students might suggest that we might hurt other people and ourselves. The craters we leave behind might not be as easy to fix as the sand.

Super Science Fact

The moon's surface has pits and craters on its surface caused by different sizes of flying debris and meteors. When mass and distance are increased, the force of impact of that object increases as well.

OBJECT	HEIGHT	DEPTH OF CRATER

Beyond the Laboratory

Truth Explosion: I can stick close to God.

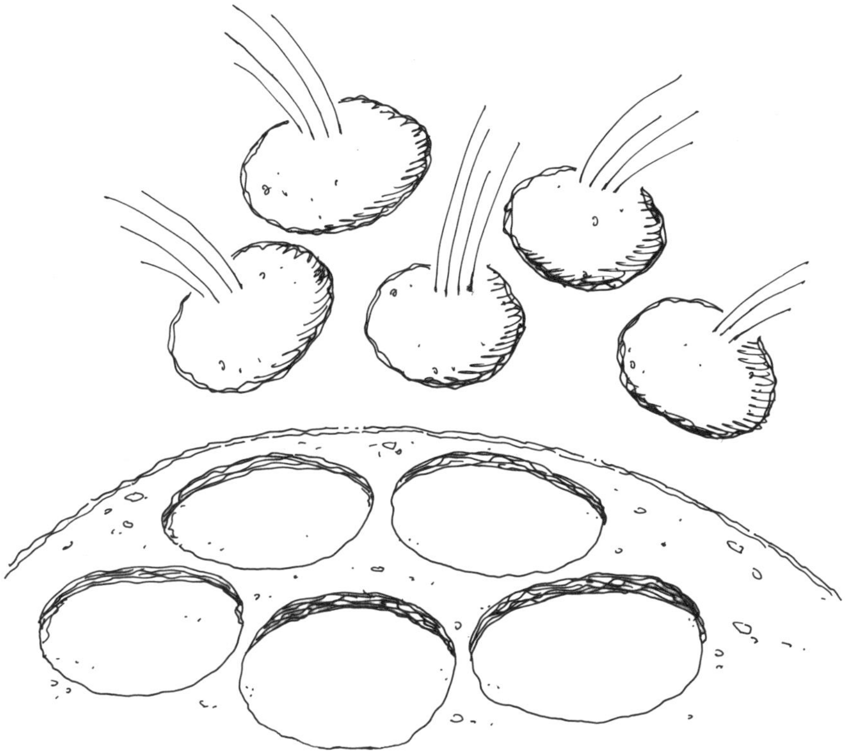

Bad decisions create big craters in our lives. Finish the picture above by labeling each meteor with the name of a sin that creates some serious damage. In the crater, write the consequences that might occur when this meteor of sin strikes the surface.

For example, a meteor like "cheating in school" can cause a crater filled with "lack of trust and poor grades."

"Let us draw near to God with a sincere heart and with the full assurance that faith brings, having our hearts sprinkled to cleanse us from a guilty conscience and having our bodies washed with pure water."
—Hebrews 10:22

"Come near to God and he will come near to you."
—James 4:8

Spread the News

Topic: Wonder
Time: 10 minutes
Group Size: Large group
Mess Meter: **1** 2 3

Great is the Lord *and most worthy of praise; his greatness no one can fathom.*
—Psalm 145:3

Formula for Success

- rulers
- table
- newspaper sheets

Your kids will want to try this experiment for themselves as they learn about the amazing world God made.

Truth Explosion: We are part of God's amazing creation.

We live in a vast "sea" of air that exerts pressure around us and on our bodies all the time. Can you feel it? Shrug your shoulders freely and encourage the kids to do the same. **Neither can I. Scientists have measured this pressure and found that our bodies can tolerate approximately 15 pounds of pressure for every square inch. But we don't feel it. God made our bodies so wonderfully that they naturally adjust to this constant pressure.**

Use this easy method to prove the presence of air pressure. Place a ruler on a table so one end hangs over the table's edge. Cover the remaining part with a single sheet of newspaper.

Point to the newspaper and ruler. **Talking about pressure, what do you think will happen to the newspaper if I put a great deal of pressure on the ruler's end? In other words, what if I went ahead and smacked the ruler's end with my fist?** (The paper will tear or fly off because the other end of the ruler will come up.)

Pause as kids respond. Then proceed with the experiment. Bring your fist sharply down on the free end of the ruler. Amazingly, the ruler will resist the blow of your fist. In fact, your strike may indeed snap the ruler without ever tearing or lifting the newspaper.

If you have extra rulers and newspaper, let kids try this activity for themselves.

Is it any wonder God made an amazing world? And that includes you and me. You're amazing! I'm amazing! This same God who created the universe cares about our bodies and minds and souls.

Genesis 1:1—2:2; Matthew 14:22–33; Mark 4:35–41

Lab Results

- **How did the results of this experiment compare with what you thought would happen?** Answers will vary.
- **Name some other amazing things about the world God made.** Answers will vary.
- **When you see the amazing way God created the world, what do you feel like saying to God?** Answers will vary.

Super Science Fact

The air pressure on the surface of the newspaper resists the sudden, upward force of the ruler. This causes the ruler to hold fast to the table.

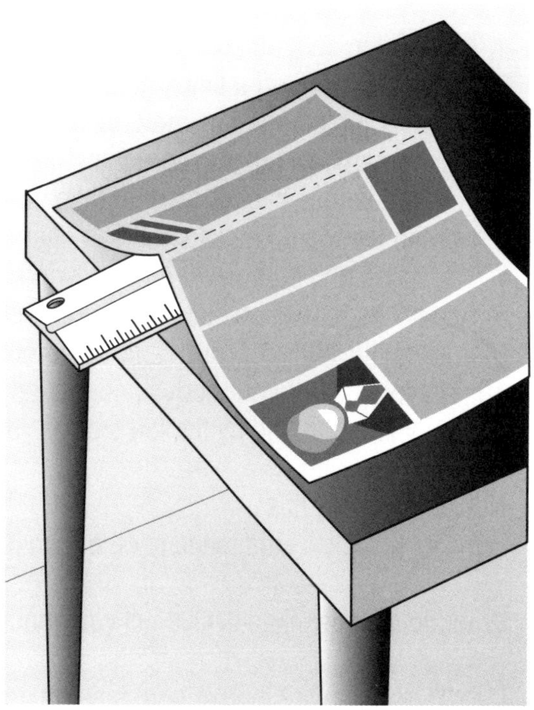

Beyond the Laboratory

Truth Explosion: We are part of God's amazing creation.

Check out these incredible facts about the bodies God gave us:

1. Laid end to end, an adult's blood vessels could circle the earth four times.
2. Our bodies give off a tiny amount of light that is too weak for the human eye to see.
3. The average person has more than 60 different kinds of bacteria in his or her bellybutton!
4. The human heart beats more than three billion times in an average lifetime.
5. Your left lung is slightly smaller than your right one.
6. Human teeth are just as strong as shark teeth.
7. Your nose and ears never stop growing.
8. As well as having unique fingerprints, humans have unique tongue prints!
9. It takes our bodies about 12 hours to completely digest food we've eaten.
10. The left side of your body is controlled by the right side of your brain, while the right side of your body is controlled by the left side of your brain.

Now think about this:
Why do you think God made each of us unique and so complex?

What do all these little details tell you about how God feels about you?

If He feels that way toward you, how do you think He feels toward the other people He created?

Knowing how God feels about the other people He created, how should you treat them?

How should you treat yourself?

Confetti Wonders

Topic: Forgiveness
Time: 10 minutes
Group Size: Individual or small groups
Mess Meter: 1 **2** 3

Bear with each other and forgive one another if any of you has a grievance against someone. Forgive as the Lord forgave you.
—Colossians 3:13

Formula for Success

- baby food jars
- cut-out confetti (the shiny kind used to decorate party tables)
- clean sand
- pitcher of water
- 2 tablespoons vegetable oil
- measuring cups and spoons

This shake up experiment will help kids see that it's possible to let go of hurt feelings and respond with forgiveness.

Truth Explosion: We can forgive each other.

Set out the supplies. If you prefer, use zip-top bags inserted into cups in place of the jars.

Have you ever had a friend you really liked—and then you had a fight? Why is it sometimes hard to separate the things we like and dislike about each other? (It's easier to focus on annoying things; if someone does something hurtful, it's hard to forget and forgive.)

We need to focus on forgiving, and on seeing the good in each other—not on the bad—although that does seem easier to do! Let's see what it takes to separate the good from the bad.

Sprinkle two teaspoons of confetti in each jar. **Let the confetti glitter represent the godly choices we make to forgive.**

Pour in two tablespoons of sand. **Sand will represent the hurts.** Fill your jar with water. **Let's finish the experiment by pouring in the oil and sealing the jars.**

How do you think the "good" feelings will separate from the "bad"?

Shake your jars! As the elements are mixed, the glitter will attach itself to the oil. The sand should remain free-floating. **After a good shake, set your jar down and watch what happens.** As the jars sit, the elements will settle—the heavier sand to the bottom, the lighter oil and confetti to the top.

Genesis 27–33, 37–45; 1 Samuel 24:1–20

God forgives us, and he wants us to forgive others. Sometimes that's hard—okay, it's always hard!—but God's way is the only way to settle things in the end.

Lab Results

- **What happened to the "good" and the "bad" in the jar?** (They separated from each other. The sand settled on the bottom and the glitter floated to the top.)
- **Do emotions have to settle before forgiveness can take place? Explain.** Answers will vary.
- **How can this experiment remind you of forgiveness?** (It will remind me that all people have good and bad in them, and that I can separate my feelings from how I respond and treat other people.)

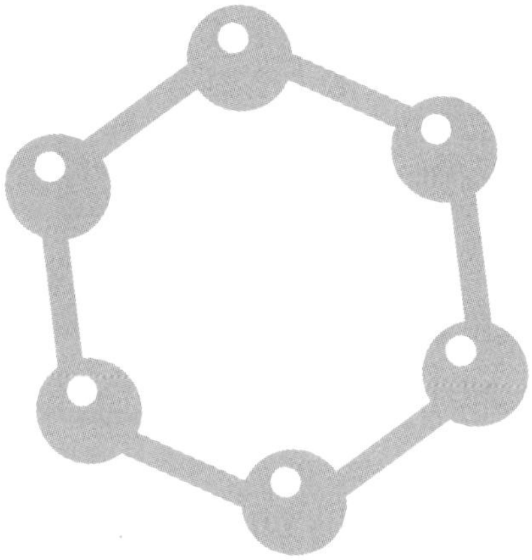

Beyond the Laboratory

Truth Explosion: We can forgive each other.

Match the phrases to complete the Scriptures.

1. "If you do not forgive others their sins,
2. "Forgive us our debts, as we
3. "Jesus said, 'Father, forgive them,
4. "For I will forgive their wickedness
5. "If we confess our sins,

a. he is faithful and just and will forgive us our sins" (1 John 1:9).
b. also have forgiven our debtors" (Matthew 6:12).
c. and will remember their sins no more" (Hebrews 8:12).
d. for they do not know what they are doing'" (Luke 23:34).
e. your Father will not forgive your sins" (Matthew 6:15).

When is it hardest for you to forgive someone?

When is it hardest for you to ask for forgiveness?

Why is it especially important for Christians to forgive?

Answers: e, b, d, c, a

A Helping Hand

Topic: Helping others
Time: 10–15 minutes
Group Size: Individuals
Mess Meter: 1 **2** 3

Let us love one another, for love comes from God. Everyone who loves has been born of God and knows God.
—1 John 4:7

Formula for Success

- plastic soda bottles (or water bottles), 1 pint to 2 liters (1 per child)
- very warm water, 105°–115° F (½ cup per child)
- yeast (1 packet per child)
- sugar (2 tablespoons per child)
- tape
- non-latex surgical gloves (1 per child)
- paper cups (3 per child)

Use this activity to help kids remember the importance of helping their families—and everyone else!

Truth Explosion: We can help each other.

Prior to your session, stretch the gloves a few times so they will quickly and easily inflate. Portion out the yeast, sugar, and water into separate paper cups for each student. Use non-latex gloves, in case a student has a latex allergy.

This activity uses warm water. To avoid having boiling water around the kids, boil the water ahead of time and pour it into a thermos. It should be the right temperature when you're ready to use it. Bring a thermometer and check it, just to be sure.

Begin the experiment by highlighting the main lesson point: **God wants us to help each other. Let's do an experiment to remind us of this.** Hold up the glove. **Our job is to blow this glove up like a balloon. But we're not going to blow into it with our mouths. What we're going to do is much more exciting.**

First, carefully pour your yeast into the bottle. Now, let's add some warm water to get things started. Have everyone pour the yeast and warm water into the bottles.

Okay, put your gloves over the top, but only the very bottom part should cover the bottle. Just hold them tightly around the opening for now. Wait a moment for kids to put the gloves over the top. **Is anything happening to the gloves?** Allow time for students to realize that nothing is happening yet. **Hmm. I guess we need a little help to make something great happen.**

Have kids take their gloves back off their bottles. Thèn have them pour the sugar into the glove. Next, the gloves should be taped tightly to the bottle top without allowing the sugar to flow down into the bottle.

Now let's try again. Have students raise the glove so the sugar falls into the bottle. If needed, help kids shake the sugar out of the gloves and into the bottles. The gloves will begin to inflate.

With a little help from the sugar, great things are happening. The yeast couldn't inflate the glove by itself; it needed the sugar's help! That's because when yeast mixes with sugar, it eats it and makes a gas called carbon dioxide. The carbon dioxide gas filled up the glove. The sugar was the yeast's helper. You can be a helper too—right in your own family and with anyone else you meet! God wants people to help each other.

Lab Results

- **How did Aaron help his brother Moses?** (He helped him by speaking for him.)
- **We saw how sugar helped yeast make carbon dioxide that filled up a glove. God put us in families so we can help each other. What are some ways you can help your family?** (by doing chores, obeying, taking care of a pet, etc.)

Super Science Fact

The process seen in this experiment is the same process that causes bread to rise. As the yeast feeds on the sugar it releases carbon dioxide gas. In our experiment, as the carbon dioxide gas rose it had nowhere to go but inside the glove. This inflated the glove like a balloon. In baking, the carbon dioxide gas is caught in the dough, forming the small bubbles as it bakes, giving bread its light and airy texture.

Beyond the Laboratory

Truth Explosion: We can help each other.

Trace the outline of your hand in the space below. Then on each finger, write a way that you can help someone else.

Beat the Wheat

Topic: Family
Time: 10–15 minutes
Group Size: Individuals
Mess Meter: 1 **2** 3

Love one another. As I have loved you, so you must love one another.
—John 13:34

Formula for Success

- wheat stalks (a few per child)
- large wooden spoons (1 per child)
- paper plates (1 per child)
- 1 cup of wheat kernels

Use this activity to help kids remember that even though families aren't perfect, God gave us families so we can love each other.

Truth Explosion: We can love our families.

Explain that threshing is the process of removing grain from the stalk and the chaff. Today, combines cut and thresh grain, but in Bible times, grain was cut by hand, then threshed by rolling a large stone over the grain or beating and separating the grain by hand.

Wheat stalks are available in most craft stores, and whole kernels of wheat can be purchased at most natural foods grocery stores. Wheat intended for craft use typically has been chemically preserved and it should not be eaten. Also, although most wheat allergies concern eating wheat, check to verify if anyone is sensitive to touching wheat.

Begin the activity with a conversation. **This is a stalk of wheat.** Hold up the wheat. **Wheat is what Ruth gathered for food to take to Naomi. We grind wheat for flour to bake bread. Where do you buy flour?** (the grocery store) **In Bible times, people couldn't buy flour at a grocery store. Why not?** (there weren't any grocery stores) **People grew wheat and made the flour themselves. In Bible times, people left some wheat in their fields so that poor people could gather it for food. Point to the stalk of wheat. Does anyone know what part of the wheat we eat?** Allow kids to guess. **We eat the kernels.** Pass around the cup of kernels. Let students feel the kernels. **But where are they? Point to the wheat stalk again. The part we eat is hidden deep inside. Before we can eat it, we have to get it out. Today we have machines to do that work, but Ruth had to do it by hand. Ruth did this by rubbing, beating, and tossing the wheat in a special way.**

Give each student a paper plate, a few stalks of wheat, and a spoon.

Have kids place the wheat on their plates then gently beat it with the back of their spoons. The kernels and the chaff will break away from the main stalk.

Now let's find the part we eat! Pick out the kernels of wheat. **What's left? It's called chaff. The chaff is so light, it blows away in the wind.** Have kids pick up some chaff in their hands and gently blow it away.

You can see how threshing wheat in Bible times would be hard work. But Ruth didn't mind doing this for Naomi because they were a family, and Ruth wanted to show Naomi she loved her. What kind of work do you do for your family? Allow a few moments for students to answer.

Lab Results

- **How did Ruth help Naomi?** (by gathering wheat)
- **Why did she help her?** (Ruth wanted to help Naomi because she was part of her family and because she loved her.)
- **What do you do to show love to your family?** (I hug them, say I love you, help them, etc.)

Super Science Fact

Wheat starts out looking like grass. That's because it's part of the grass family, just like rice, barley, and oats. As it grows it produces a plume at the top that contains the kernels of wheat. The kernels of wheat are also seeds, and if planted, will grow into more wheat. Otherwise, we can grind the kernels to make flour once we get them out of the stalk, or husk or chaff. Removing the kernels is called threshing.
In Bible times, wheat was threshed, or separated from the husk or chaff, by rubbing it between your hands, rolling a large stone over it, or beating it against something. All these ways caused the chaff to come apart and separate from the kernels. The chaff is very light and the kernels are heavier. A little wind blows the lighter husk away from the heavier kernels. Today, machines make this job easy and efficient. After the kernels are removed the stalks can be used as bedding for farm animals. We call this straw.

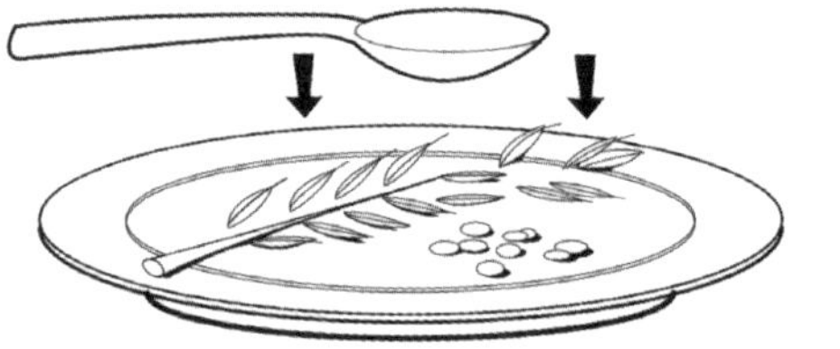

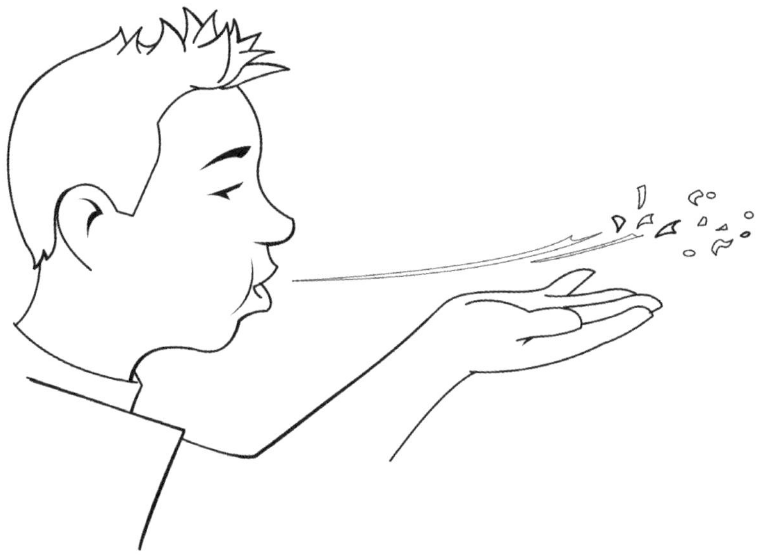

Beyond the Laboratory

Truth Explosion: We can love our families.

Finish these sentences about your family.

The thing I like best about my family is …

Some things my family likes to do together are …

My family is special because …

I like to help my family by …

In my family, I can do a better job of …

Body Beautiful

Topic: Discernment
Time: 25 minutes
Group Size: Small groups
Mess Meter: 1 **2** 3

I have chosen the way of faithfulness;
I have set my heart on your laws.
—Psalm 119:30

Formula for Success

- play dough (or soft clay)
- zip-top bags
- cornstarch
- light corn syrup
- yellow food coloring
- water
- measuring cup
- cotton swabs

Kids get an earful as they learn about the importance of listening to good advice.

Truth Explosion: We can help each other make good decisions.

We use our ears to hear a variety of vibrations. Bells, whistles, music, car engines, voices …

What noises do you hear on your way to school each day?

With so much going on, how well do we really hear? In other words, how well do we listen? There's an expression that sums up this thought nicely. Raise your ear if you've heard the expression—"in one ear and out the other." Pause as kids try to raise their ears! **Exactly! It's as if our ears are stopped up and we can't hear what we need to hear.** Pass out the play dough. **I'd like you to use the play dough to sculpt an ear. Be sure to make it as large as possible because next you'll make earwax!**

Have kids work in groups for both the ears and the cornstarch "wax." Or you can measure ingredients for kids to make individual batches. The basic recipe is one-half cup of cornstarch and one-fourth cup of light corn syrup. Put these ingredients in the zip-top bag and add a few drops of water and yellow food coloring. Knead the bag to mix everything together. Multiply or divide the recipe as appropriate for your group. When everyone has a sculpted ear and a bag of "wax," distribute the cotton swabs.

Hold up a sculpted ear. **Now suppose this is your ear. And you're in a situation where you need some wise advice. But the wise advice you hear means you can't do what you want or you have to do something very hard. Do you "tune out" and choose not to pay attention? Use your cotton swabs to fill your play dough ears with earwax.**

1 Samuel 13:1–15; 1 Kings 12:1–19; Esther 2:1—9:17

As kids work have them share with their neighbors times when others "tune" them out and how that makes them feel.

Good vibrations equal good advice! When we refuse to listen to good advice, it's like we've stopped up our ears. But God sends us wise people who give us good advice. They're truly a blessing! So let's listen up and do our best to pay attention.

Lab Results

- **Who can you trust to give you good advice in tough situations?** (my parents, close friends, Christian adults, my teachers, our youth minister, siblings, and so on)

- **What are some ways you stop up your ears if you get advice you really don't want to hear?** (I ignore what the person says; I listen but don't respond; I change the subject or avoid the person; I get angry.)

- **How can we unstop our ears so we can listen to good advice?** (We can remember God put people in our lives for a reason, and He wants us to take care of each other. We can put our own pride and selfishness aside and think about what God wants us to do.)

Super Science Fact

The process seen in this experiment is the same process that causes bread to rise. As the yeast feeds on the sugar it releases carbon dioxide gas. In our experiment, as the carbon dioxide gas rose it had nowhere to go but inside the glove. This inflated the glove like a balloon. In baking, the carbon dioxide gas is caught in the dough, forming the small bubbles as it bakes, giving bread its light and airy texture.

Beyond the Laboratory

Truth Explosion: We can help each other make good decisions.

Read these bits of advice and do your best to explain what they mean.

A bird in the hand is worth two in the bush.

Early to bed, early to rise makes a man healthy, wealthy, and wise.

Grin and bear it.

A penny saved is a penny earned.

Better late than never.

Now read each of the following proverbs from the Bible and put them in your own words. When might this advice be helpful to you or others?

"The Lord disciplines those he loves, as a father the son he delights in."
—Proverbs 3:12

"A gentle answer turns away wrath, but a harsh word stirs up anger."
—Proverbs 15:1

"The greedy stir up conflict, but those who trust in the Lord will prosper."
—Proverbs 28:25

"Whoever is patient has great understanding, but one who is quick-tempered displays folly."
—Proverbs 14:29

"A friend loves at all times, and a brother is born for a time of adversity."
—Proverbs 17:17

Tongue Teasers

Topic: The impact of words
Time: 15–20 minutes
Group Size: Small groups
Mess Meter: **1** 2 3

Out of the same mouth come praise and cursing. My brothers and sisters, this should not be.
—James 3:10

Formula for Success

- orange juice
- toothpaste containing sodium lauryl sulfate
- several new toothbrushes
- water for rinsing

This little part of the body can have a painful bite. No, not the teeth … the tongue! Kids will find out if their tongue brings out the best—or worst—in others.

Truth Explosion: We can think before we speak.

Two out of three people have inherited a bitterness-detecting gene. When a certain chemical comes in contact with the citric acid in orange juice—wow! It increases the bitter taste tenfold. Find out which kids in your group have this gene by doing a little experiment with toothpaste and orange juice.

Did you know that some of you have inherited a certain gene that allows you to taste bitterness? That's right—some of your tongues are ready to turn on you at a moment's notice! In fact, two out of every three people have tongues that can detect a bitter taste when they put certain foods or chemicals in their mouths. Do you think you're one of them? Let's find out!

Choose some volunteers. If you have a large group, select two or three kids to give this a try in front of the class. Tell the others they can try this at home. If you have a smaller group, provide enough toothbrushes for everyone to try the activity.

Have the volunteers brush their teeth—but tell them not to rinse too thoroughly when they're done. The more residue from the toothpaste left in the mouth, the stronger the effect when they taste the orange juice. Then have each one take a sip of orange juice.

So what do you think? How does it taste? There is a chemical in some toothpastes that reacts to the acid in a glass of orange juice, and the result is ... well, you can tell us better than I can!

Lab Results

- **For being so small, the tongue is a pretty amazing part of our body. Do you know the four main tastes humans can detect?** (sweet, salty, sour, and bitter)
- **The Bible tells us the tongue can be sweet or it can be deadly. How can something like a tongue actually be dangerous?** (The things we say can hurt people. We can gossip, tell lies, criticize, or even curse. All of these deadly things come out of our mouths.)
- **On the other hand, the Bible says the our tongue can "bring life." What does that mean?** (We are able to encourage each other, praise God with our singing and worship, speak the truth, and show love with our words.)

Super Science Fact

A gene is the basic cellular unit that is responsible for what we physically inherit from our parents. Sodium lauryl sulfate is a harmless chemical found in many household detergents, toothpaste and some mouthwash. Our taste buds can detect four basic tastes: sweet, salty, sour, and bitter.

Beyond the Laboratory

Truth Explosion: We can think before we speak.

Gather your Bibles and let's go!

1. The Bible compares our speech (the tongue) to many different things. See if your group can find out what these verses say about our speech:

The tongue is like a ______________________________ (Psalm 52:2).

The tongue is like a ______________________________ (Proverbs 15:4).

The tongue is like a ______________________________ (James 3:5–6).

The tongue is like a ______________________________ (James 3:8).

The tongue is like a ______________________________ (Proverbs 25:23).

2. Can you remember a time when someone's words really hurt you or someone else you knew? Go around your group, and if you're comfortable, share about a time when you saw for yourself just how powerful someone's words could be.

3. Can you recall a time when someone said something to you that made you feel amazing? What did the person say, and how did it make you feel?

4. For each situation, write a life-giving comment. In other words, what is something you could say with your mouth that would encourage and build up?

   Your friend's cat is missing, and he or she is feeling upset.
   Your sister just got cut from the volleyball team.
   Your mom is tired after a long day, and she asks you to help her make dinner.
   A friend turns to you and says, "Do you know what I just heard about …?"

Look up Proverbs 21:23. Write it down and memorize it!

Answers: e, b, d, c, a

Cool It

Topic: Kindness, anger
Time: 15–20 minutes
Group Size: Small groups
Mess Meter: **1** 2 3

A gentle answer turns away wrath, but a harsh word stirs up anger.
—Proverbs 15:1

Formula for Success

- candle in a sturdy holder
- beaker or glass cup
- spoonful of baking soda
- vinegar

Can't control that anger? With the mix of a few common ingredients, we will find the worst flames begin to flicker out.

Truth Explosion: We can choose kindness over anger.

During this experiment, make it very clear that adults should always be present when using fire for any task. Even with a mature group, you will want to be in charge of this entire process. During the simple experiment, you will be demonstrating a principle of fire—using an ordinary gas to smother a flame on contact.

What is the first thing that comes to your mind when you think of fire? Listen to responses. **Whether it's a raging inferno or a small candle, all fires operate on the same principle.**

A fire needs three things to survive. Does anybody know what they are? A fire needs fuel, oxygen, and some kind of spark. If one of those isn't present, the fire will go out.

Today we're going to see what happens when one of those three things is removed. Only an adult can do this experiment, so don't do this at home unless your parent can help you.

Use a match to light your candle. (You can explain to the kids that the match creates the first requirement of fire: a spark.) Next, measure one spoonful of baking soda into your water glass and add a splash of vinegar—enough to create a foaming reaction in the glass.

Proverbs 15:1; 16:32; Ecclesiastes 10:4

As soon as the mixture stops foaming, tip the glass over the flame, as if you're pouring the water onto the wick. Don't actually pour anything onto the candle—make sure you just place the opening of the glass above the flame. The flame will go out, even if the air is completely still.

Lab Results

- **Why do you think the flame went out?** (The gas created by the baking soda smothered the flame.)

- **How is anger a lot like fire?** (Anger can burn out of control. Sometimes we even call it being "hot-tempered.") **Have you ever felt your anger spark inside of you?** Responses will vary.

- **When you're angry, what can make your anger worse?** (Anger can grow out of control when someone starts to fight back or you strike out with yelling or hitting. That's like putting more fuel on the fire. Other responses will vary.)

- **What can make your anger start to go out?** (Anger can be softened with an apology, a kind word, a time-out, or even talking it out with someone you trust.)

- **What does the Bible say about anger? Listen to Proverbs 15:1: "A gentle answer turns away wrath, but a harsh word stirs up anger." What does this mean?** (When someone tries to pick a fight with you or responds in anger, you can help "put out the flame" by being kind instead.)

Super Science Fact

A fire needs oxygen in order to survive. Carbon dioxide gas smothers a fire because it prevents contact between the fire and oxygen.

Beyond the Laboratory

Truth Explosion: We can choose kindness over anger.

Get ready to discover some truth about anger! Look up the following verses in the Bible and answer the questions. Be ready to report back to the group.

Proverbs 15:1

What effect can our spoken response have on an angry person?

How can we practice this verse in our everyday lives?

Proverbs 16:32

What's better than being a warrior?

What's better than "taking a city"?

Even though it's hard, what can we gain by being patient?

Ecclesiastes 10:4

What is often our first reaction when someone strikes out in anger at us?

What does this verse say we should do instead?

What will happen if we do?

Ephesians 4:31

What does the word *slander* mean? (If you don't know, ask your teacher or look it up.)

Copy the list of things this verse says we should avoid in our speech.

Stretching the Truth

Topic: Honesty
Time: 15–20 minutes
Group Size: Pairs
Mess Meter: **1** 2 3

Therefore each of you must put off falsehood and speak truthfully to your neighbor, for we are all members of one body.
—Ephesians 4:25

Formula for Success

- several pieces of stiff cardboard (the size of a business card is about right)
- your lips
- a friend

Are you honest—or do you like to stretch the truth? When the truth gets crooked, we can't always tell when something's up or down. Stretching our lips out of alignment gives us a freaky illustration about truth and falsehood.

Truth Explosion: We can tell the truth.

This experiment shows how easily it is for our lips to lie to us. Using sense memory, your group will be able to "trick" the nerve endings in their lips. This experiment is a dynamite illustration about appearance versus reality. You will want to practice this on yourself first so you can take your kids through the experiment easily.

Believe it or not, your fingertips or tickly stomach aren't the most touch-sensitive parts of your body. It's actually your lips! You will be amazed at how much your lips have learned in your short life. Get ready to be amazed!

You will need a friend to do this experiment, so find a buddy. One person will close his or her eyes while the other person slips the corner of a small piece of cardboard against the partner's lips—one edge touching the top lip and the other edge touching the bottom lip, like this (demonstrate for the kids). **Hold the cardboard between your lips.**

While your eyes are closed, tell your partner whether the card is straight up and down or tilted right or left at an angle. Chances are you'll get it right every time.

Let pairs try this out on each other. Make sure you have plenty of cards on hand so kids don't share germs!

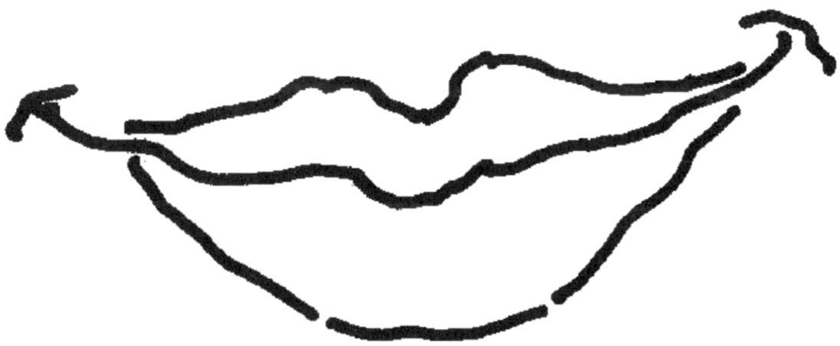

Are you ready to fix it so that your lips will lie to you?

Pull your own lips crossways—one going right and one going left. You can gently tug at the skin right under your lips to make it easy.

Close your eyes. This time, let your partner position the card vertically, straight up and down, touching both your lips. Wow! What does it feel like? No matter how straight the card, the brain relays a message that it's tilted.

Lab Results

- **Why do you think your lips lied to you?** Answers will vary.
- **The longer we go on believing something false, the harder it is to change our thinking! What does this say about the importance of knowing the difference between truth and lies?** (If we keep listening to false things, we might end up believing they're really true.)
- **What kinds of lies do some kids start believing? What do you hear at school or on television that might be untrue?** Listen to answers. Some kids might want to bring up rumors while others might want to point out crazy misinformation about the nature of God, moral absolutes, or the Bible's teaching.

Super Science Fact

A lifetime of nerve messages makes your brain expect certain messages. Pull your lips out of alignment, and in the absence of vision, your brain will assume the wrong message. The brain actually adjusts over time. One scientist had a man wear special glasses that made everything appear upside down. After three weeks, his brain had adjusted to the glasses and when he took them off, the world was backwards! Fortunately, the result wasn't permanent.

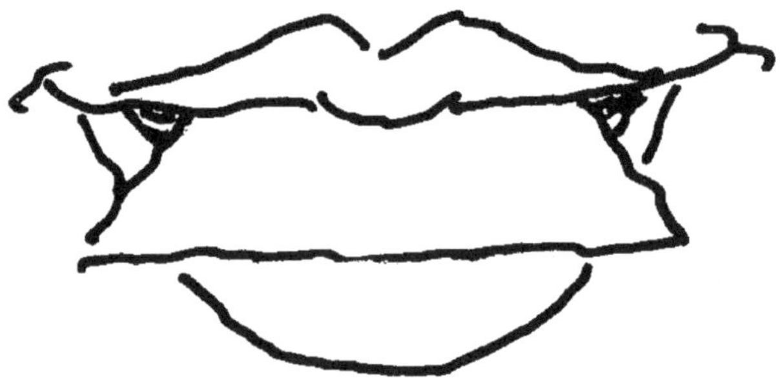

Beyond the Laboratory

Truth Explosion: We can tell the truth.

1. What do you think kids your age are tempted to lie about the most? Write down some of your ideas.

2. We know God doesn't want us to lie. Psalm 34:13 tells us to keep our tongue from evil and our lips from speaking lies. But why? What would you say to someone who says that a little "stretching the truth" doesn't hurt anybody?

3. God isn't the only one who thinks that honesty is important. Other people will respect a person who will not spread lies. What does Proverbs 16:13 say? Put this verse into your own words and write it down.

Which comes first? Here's the truth. When we lie, bad stuff starts to happen. Look at the six items below and place its color label in the correct spot on the "lying cycle." Which comes first? What consequences follow from that?

BLUE: Stephanie forgets her math homework and asks to copy someone else's answers.
YELLOW: Stephanie's teacher calls her mom and dad and they find out she lied.
GREEN: Stephanie's teacher asks her if she cheated, and she says, "No way."
BLACK: Stephanie has lost her parents' and her teacher's trust, and she must serve detention for her bad decision.
ORANGE: Stephanie didn't do her own work, so she is not prepared for the test and earns a D.
RED: Stephanie wants to earn a better grade in math.

Answers: e, b, d, c, a

The Power of a Few Good Friends

Topic: Friendship
Time: 15–20 minutes
Group Size: Small groups
Mess Meter: **1** 2 3

If we love one another, God lives in us and his love is made complete in us.
—1 John 4:12

Formula for Success

- keys on a key ring
- 3 paper clips
- pen or pencil
- 1 yard of string

The burdens of the world may try to drag you down, but a few friends can help you win the battle. Kids see how a small object can stop a heavy one from falling—with the power of friction.

Truth Explosion: We can support each other as friends.

From about sixth grade, kids start to feel the power of friendships grow exponentially. As they begin to hit life's rough patches, friendships can become an asset or a liability. In this experiment, your students will be able to visualize the effect that a smaller weight can have on a bigger one. In the process, it will give you an opportunity to discuss the importance of "breaking a fall" when a friend might be crashing to the ground.

You already know about gravity. It's the force that keeps our bodies from flying away every morning, and the power to keep us sticking to our beds every night. Gravity seems pretty powerful, right? Let's do a little trick with a pencil and some keys. It's not too complicated, but it will teach us a thing or two about gravity and friction.

You will need to tie the ring of keys to one end of the string and the paper clips to the other end. Have two students hold a pencil horizontally, each person holding one end. Drape the string over the pencil so that the keys are hanging down. Only about one-third of the string should be hanging down, and the other two-thirds should be horizontal as you hold it straight out.

Proverbs 17:17; 25:13; Ecclesiastes 4:9–10

Which end is heavier? What do you think is going to happen when I let go of the string? Let's find out!

Obviously, the keys will drop. But surprisingly, they'll never reach the ground. The paper clips spin around the pencil, winding the string. By the time the string wraps around the pencil six times, it will break the fall of the keys.

Lab Results

- **Gravity is so cool. When do you see gravity working in your everyday life?** (We see gravity when leaves fall off of trees, during rainfall, when someone trips, when we play baseball, and so forth. Your kids will come up with many examples.)
- **When we start to fall, how can friends be a lot like the paper clips on the end of the string?** (Friends can be the force that keeps us from crashing—whether they encourage us to keep going, teach us God's Word, or listen when we're upset.)
- **Sometimes friends aren't enough to keep someone from getting hurt. Who else can we turn to if we feel like we're falling away from God?** (We can turn to our parents, brothers and sisters, teachers, or pastors.)

Super Science Fact

Friction is the force that resists motion between two surfaces. Gravity pulls the heavier weight (the keys) with greater force. But the friction between the string and the pencil stops the motion.

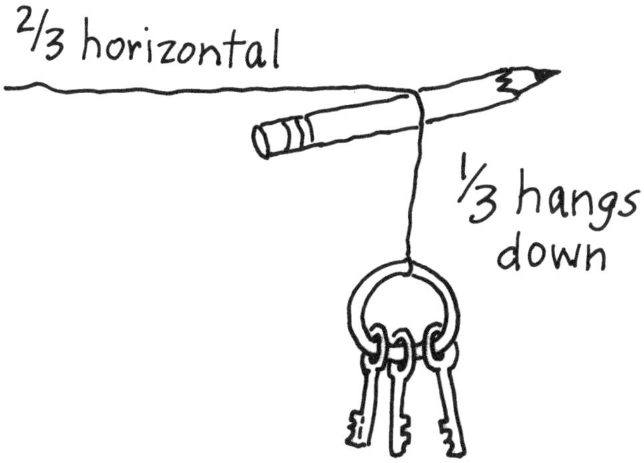

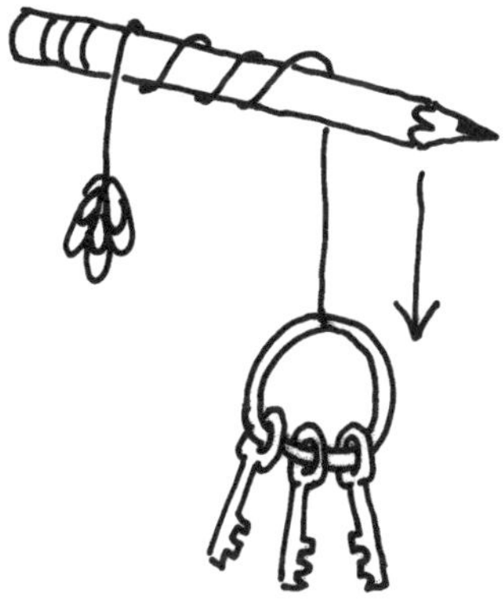

Beyond the Laboratory

Truth Explosion: We can support each other as friends.

1. Find a partner. One of you will be the interviewer and the other will be the interviewee.

Interview Questions →	Responses
Can you think of one time when a good friend helped you get out of a real mess?	
If you noticed that a good friend was really having a hard time obeying God's commands, what would you do about it? →	

Interviewers, write down your partner's responses. Then get with a few other kids to form a small group.

2. In your small group, do some Bible investigation. Find the following verses in your Bible and read them out loud to each other.

Proverbs 17:17
Proverbs 25:13
Ecclesiastes 4:9–10

Tell your group what you learned about friendship from these verses.

Let's Just Stick Together

Topic: Faithfulness
Time: 15–20 minutes
Group Size: Small groups
Mess Meter: 1 2 **3**

By this everyone will know that you are my disciples, if you love one another.
—John 13:35

Formula for Success

- borax
- paper cups
- plain white school glue
- food coloring
- wooden sticks for stirring

If we isolate ourselves from others, we're just not that strong. Kids will discover that when they bond with a good friend or two, they'll begin to stretch themselves!

Truth Explosion: We can build strong friendships.

Why do kids like gooey things? The sticky, slippery, stretchy qualities of polymers have fascinated kids forever, whether they're playing in the mud on a summer day, making silly putty stick to furniture or molding modeling clay into shapes.

In this activity, your kids get to make their own polymers, finding out how certain ingredients stick together to form new, bondable substances. In the process, they will illustrate the nature of friendship as God designed it.

Who likes to chew gum? Have you ever made something out of baking clay? What about stepping into tar or asphalt on a hot day? All of these are examples of a scientific term called a polymer. A long time ago, people had to make things out of glass, metal, paper, or wood. But now, we use plastic—an important polymer made up of manmade, bonded ingredients.

Today you get to make your own sticky substance! You will get a little messy, so get ready!

Mix together two spoonfuls of water with two spoonfuls of borax in a paper cup. You will want to fill as many paper cups as you have kids—or prepare a cup for each pair of kids. Once the kids have stirred this together, add a spoonful of white glue. This will form a putty-like substance that is easy to stretch and play with! You can also add primary colors to the mixture, giving each pair of kids a different shade of putty.

Proverbs 18:24; John 15:12

Lab Results

- **Look around the room. What are some things you can see that are made from manmade plastic?** (Bowls, synthetic tables, chairs, and toys are all things from manmade materials.)

- **Plastics are made up of different building blocks that bond together—kind of like the putty material you made today. Do you think we could separate the glue from the water mixture after we've stirred it up? Why not?** (Once you combine them, they bond together permanently.)

- **How is a Christian friendship a little like our stretchy, gooey creation?** (A good friendship sticks together. Friends "stretch" you. They might even be colorful!)

- **Does God want us to have Christian friends? Why?** (Christian friends usually have the same beliefs. They understand you and will encourage you to make good decisions.)

Super Science Fact

A polymer is a large, complex molecule built from smaller molecules joined together. Natural polymers are things like fingernails and spider webs. Synthetic polymers are things like carpets, clothing, glue, and chewing gum.

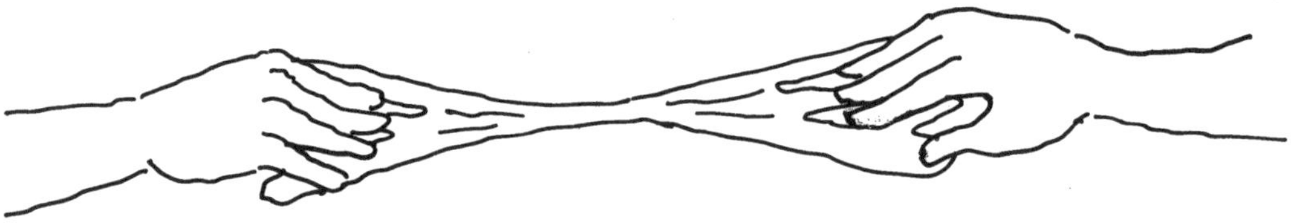

Beyond the Laboratory

Truth Explosion: We can build strong friendships.

Friends are so important! Some friendships are about fun and companionship. Others are more about competition and activities. Perhaps you even have friends who can know a lot about you—even your faults—and still give you love and patience.

1. Write down a description of the type of friend listed in each box. Ask your teacher for ideas if you need help. The first one is done for you, but you might have more ideas.

Activity Friends *belonging to the same sports team *enjoying a hobby or attending a club together *attending the same dance class	Acquaintances
Family Friends	Your "Best" Friend

2. Could a friend be part of more than one box? Do you have any friends like that?

3. Read the following verse taken from Proverbs 18:24:

"One who has unreliable friends soon comes to ruin, but there is a friend who sticks closer than a brother."

Does God expect us to be best friends with everyone we meet? What do you think the Bible means by a "true friend"? Why is it so important to find the right kinds of friends? Will a good friend sometimes hurt you? When have you ever hurt a friend?

4. Read John 15:12 in your Bible. What does Jesus command us to do? Is it hard to love others the way Jesus asks us to? How can God help us follow this commandment?

Sweet Service

Topic: Serving others
Time: 10–15 minutes
Group Size: Large group
Mess Meter: 1 2 **3**

[Jesus] went around doing good.
—Acts 10:38

Formula for Success

- large coffee can with lid
- ¼ cup milk
- ¼ cup whipping cream
- 4 tablespoons sugar
- ¼ teaspoon vanilla
- quart-sized zippered freezer bag
- crushed ice
- rock salt
- spoons (1 per child)

Use this tasty activity to remind children of the importance of humbly serving others.

Truth Explosion: We can serve one another.

This recipe makes enough for about 20 small bites of ice cream. If you have a larger class, make more than one can of ice cream. Don't double the recipe in a larger bag and can. It will take longer to freeze.

It's possible the salt solution involved in this experiment may leak from the can and damage flooring. Plan on doing this activity outside or cover the floor where the students will be working.

Always check with parents for allergies before serving food to your students. If a student is sensitive to dairy products, ask if you can offer some sorbet as an alternative treat at the end or lactose free ice cream.

Let's play a game and do an experiment at the same time! Pour one-quarter cup of milk, one-quarter cup of whipping cream, four tablespoons sugar, and a teaspoon of vanilla into a zippered freezer bag. Close the bag tightly. Place bag inside another zippered freezer bag and close it tightly as well.

Layer ice and salt until the can is about one third full. Place the full zippered bag into the coffee can. Layer ice and salt in the remainder of the coffee can, and place the lid securely on top.

Sit in a large circle with your class. **Jesus taught that we should serve others. Let's roll this can to each other. When the can comes to you, name a way you can serve others.** Roll the can across the floor, making sure each student has the opportunity to share. Roll the can for about seven to ten minutes. When the ice cream is frozen, the can will become difficult to roll.

What did Jesus say would happen when we serve others? (we become important, good things happen) **Let's see if something good happened as we rolled the can.** Open the can and remove enough ice to retrieve the zippered bag. **Our ingredients turned into a smooth creamy treat!**

Dip out samples and serve each student a tasty bite. **Something good always happens when we learn to serve others!**

Lab Results

- **What did Jesus say James and John had to do to become important?** (serve others, be kind and helpful)

- **How can you serve others?** Answers will vary.

Super Science Fact

It's cooking! And it's science too! Heating and cooling are really just moving energy (heat) from one place to another. For something to cook, it must absorb energy. For milk to freeze into ice cream, something else has to take its energy away. In this case, the ice takes the energy away. Salt lowers the freezing point of the ice so that the energy is absorbed more quickly.

Beyond the Laboratory

Truth Explosion: We can serve one another.

Use the letters in the word SERVE to list five things you can do for others this week.

S

E

R

V

E

How was Jesus a servant?

Why was Jesus a servant?

How can you be a servant, and why is it important?

Blow Me Over Hope

Topic: Hope
Time: 15 minutes
Group Size: Individual
Mess Meter: **1** 2 3

But you, Lord, are a compassionate and gracious God, slow to anger, abounding in love and faithfulness.
—Psalm 86:15

Formula for Success

- index cards
- pencils
- table

Pair feelings of hopelessness with that of compassion. Allow your kids to see how one needs the caring action of the other.

Truth Explosion: We can show we care.

"Take your time."

"It's about time."

"I don't have time."

"Time's up."

We have 101 expressions about time—something that we can't feel or hold in our hands.

For example, do you get a little nervous when it's time to go to school and you can't find your shoes, backpack, homework, or lunch money? As we all know, school buses wait for no one! And do your parents make it worse when they ask you to make up time and get moving?

Have volunteers share times that leave them pressured, discouraged, and overwhelmed.

Pass out the index cards. **Now it's your turn! On your card write or draw a time that is an everyday discouragement, one that makes you feel at odds with the world. Maybe it's getting up in the morning, doing your math homework, or facing a sink full of greasy dishes.** Allow kids to draw or write. Go ahead and pick up a pencil and make a drawing of your own.

Now flip the card and draw or write your favorite time of day—time filled with relaxation and the feeling that you have "all the time in the world." When kids finish, demonstrate how to gently bend the index card and set it on the table. Make sure the discouraging side faces out.

Luke 8:40–42, 49–56; 10:25–37; 17:11–19; John 5:1–15

Now try to flip your card by blowing on it. This may look easy, but it's not. Even when kids blow above or below the card, the card should not flip.

So sorry! I set you up for that. I knew it was hopeless, but I did it to prove a point. Can anyone tell me what that is? Allow time for kids to respond. **Very good! When we or those around us feel hopeless, Jesus can help. Always.**

Jesus healed a lot of people when it seemed hopeless—even raising some from the dead. We can show others we care by sharing the hope that comes from knowing our Savior.

Lab Results

- **What do you do when you feel hopeless? What makes you feel better?** Answers will vary, but may include the following: I talk to a friend, go for a walk, listen to music, pray, work out, and so on.
- **How can Jesus help you when things seem hopeless?** (He helps me remember that there is more to life that what is happening right now; reminds me that everything will turn out all right in the end; gives me strength that I don't have on my own.)
- **How can you give hope to someone else by sharing the love of Jesus?** (I can help other people understand that God loves them and will be with them through whatever they face; I can show them God has a plan and their problems are only temporary; and so on.)

Super Science Fact

A polymer is a large, complex molecule built from smaller molecules joined together. Natural polymers are things like fingernails and spider webs. Synthetic polymers are things like carpets, clothing, glue, and chewing gum.

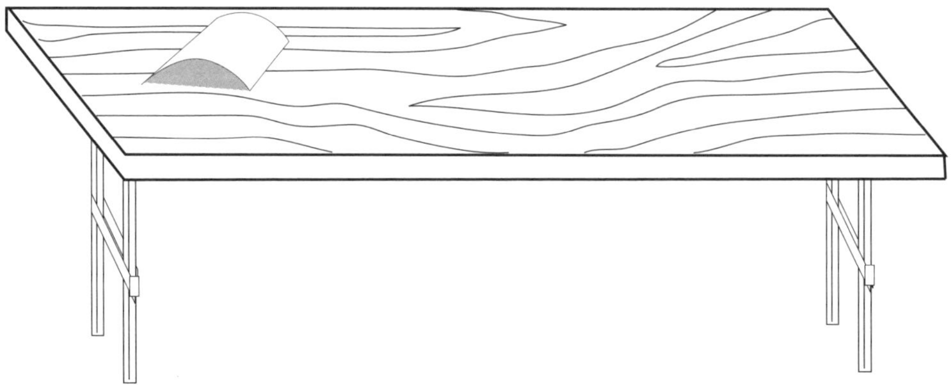

Beyond the Laboratory

Truth Explosion: We can show we care.

"For now we see only a reflection as in a mirror; then we shall see face to face.
Now I know in part; then I shall know fully, even as I am fully known.
And now these three remain: faith, hope and love.
But the greatest of these is love."
—1 Corinthians 13:12–13

Write your own definitions for each of these words:

faith:

hope:

love:

Use the space below to design a symbol that represents one or all of these concepts. As you work, think about what faith, hope, and love have in common and how you can share those things with someone who is hurting.

A Chance of Clouds

Topic: Worship
Time: 10 minutes
Group Size: Groups of four
Mess Meter: 1 **2** 3

You are worthy, our Lord and God, to receive glory and honor and power.
—Revelation 4:11

Formula for Success

- hot water
- metal dishes
- clear jars
- ice cubes
- small action figures

As kids make a cloud in a jar, they'll see God's power and remember that He is worthy of worship.

Truth Explosion: We can lead others to know and worship Jesus.

As you begin this activity, or a little ahead of time, fill the metal dishes with ice cubes. Kids will need to see this up close, so plan on a dish and jar for about every four kids. Let the ice cubes chill the dish thoroughly.

Before Jesus went to heaven, He told His followers to tell other people the good news that they can be part of God's kingdom. Then Jesus rose into a cloud. Let's make a cloud in a jar to remind us that as Jesus went to heaven, He gave all His followers a job to do.

Set an action figure behind each glass. Have the kids look through the clear glass to see the action figure on the other side. Point out how clearly they can see. Then add one inch of hot tap water in the jar.

When the metal dish is cold, remove the ice from the dish. Immediately place the metal dish over the top of the jar, cold side down. As the hot water evaporates, it will come in contact with the cold dish. The moisture will condense and form a cloud. **Scientifically speaking, we'll see warm water evaporate into the air where it will be met by cold air, causing condensation. Mini-clouds!** Ask kids to look through the glass again. This time the cloud will obscure their vision of the action figure. Let kids repeat the experiment as time allows.

Another way to do this activity is to tape black paper on the back of a jar and pour in some warm water. Hold a lit match in the jar for a few seconds and then drop it in. Quickly cover the jar opening with an ice pack. Water droplets will cling to the trail of manmade smoke for a mini-cloud formation.

God wants the whole world to know Him and worship Him. That's why Jesus sent the disciples

Matthew 17:1–8; Acts 1:1–11

to the ends of the earth to spread the good news. And now it's our turn. Let's make Jesus' message crystal clear to those we meet.

Lab Results

- **What job was Jesus preparing the disciples for?** (to tell others about Him)
- **What did the disciples see the last time they were together with Jesus?** (They saw the ascension. Jesus was hidden by a cloud.)
- **When has watching the clouds made you feel amazed at God's power?** Answers will vary.
- **How can we carry on the same job the disciples were doing?** (We can tell others about what Jesus means to us; we can invite other people to church; we can be kind and loving to others as Jesus was.)

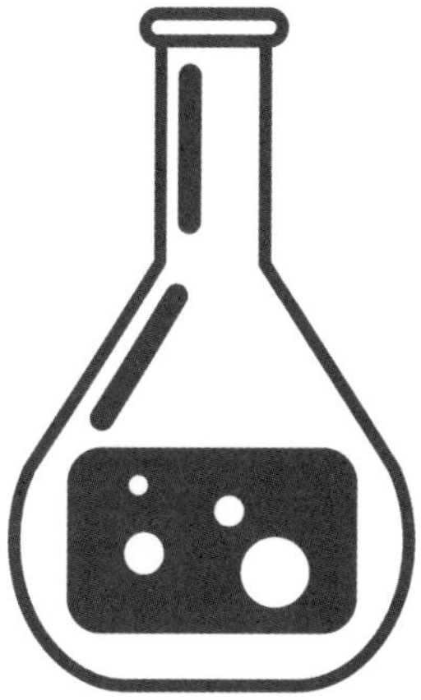

Beyond the Laboratory

Truth Explosion: We can lead others to know and worship Jesus.

For each group or individual below, name the person who is the leader.

baseball team ______________________________

marching band ______________________________

class of students ______________________________

construction crew ______________________________

United States ______________________________

police department ______________________________

fast food restaurant ______________________________

Have you ever been a leader?

What did you like about being a leader? What did you dislike?

List below some ways that you can lead someone to Jesus:

1.

2.

3.

Circle the way that you would most like to try, and then ask God to help you.

A Colorful Spread

Topic: Evangelism
Time: 10 minutes
Group Size: Groups of four
Mess Meter: **1** 2 3

But you will receive power when the Holy Spirit comes on you; and you will be my witnesses in Jerusalem, and in all Judea and Samaria, and to the ends of the earth.
—Acts 1:8

Formula for Success

- round cake pans
- whole milk (warmed)
- food coloring
- dishwashing liquid

Let your kids see how fast they can spread the good news while they watch swirling colors speed across a milky world.

Truth Explosion: We can carry on the work of God's kingdom.

Jesus wants us to be His witnesses to the very ends of the earth. Point to the cake pans. **The round cake pans represent our round Earth. Let's see what we can do to spread the news of Jesus.**

Gather kids in groups of four around the cake pans. Have kids pour milk into the cake pans to a one-inch depth. Choose a food color to represent "witnesses." Let each group of students choose a color.

Take turns squeezing a drop of food coloring near the edge of the pan.

Have kids gently squeeze one drop of dishwashing liquid on top of the food color spots. Watch the witnesses go! The food coloring will instantly "spread out" and erupt into colorful swirls. Keep watching. The colors will eventually disperse throughout the cake pans.

When we put our faith in Jesus, He gives us what we need to spread the good news to others. We have the Holy Spirit living in us, ready to take us to the ends of the earth.

God gives us the great gift of salvation, and He wants us to help others receive the gift too. He sent the Holy Spirit to help us do the job. Spread the news!

Something Extra!

Pour milk or water into a bowl. Take a paper clip and place it on the tines of a fork. Gently place the paper clip, as level as possible, on the surface of the liquid. Once the paper clip floats, add one drop of dish soap. Oops! Watch as the clip falls to the bottom of the dish. (Fun Science Fact: The detergent disrupts the surface tension of the liquid.)

Matthew 4:18–22; Luke 3:1–18; 5:1–11; 6:12–16; Acts 2:1–12

Lab Results

- **How should we be like the fast-acting dishwashing liquid?** (We should spread out and make a difference in the world around us.)

- **What does a "witness for Christ" mean to you?** (showing others what Jesus is like by the way we live, telling others the good news about Him)

- **Name two ways you can be a witness "to the ends of the earth."** Answers will vary, but may include giving money to missionaries, praying for people around the world, and doing what I can to make a difference in my own corner of the world.

Super Science Fact

The detergent breaks up the fat globules in the "resting" milk. As the globules break and expand, they create movement in the milk, allowing the food coloring to spread across the surface of the milk.

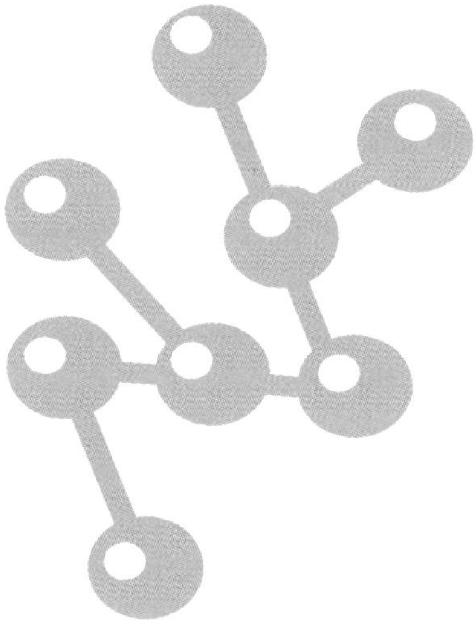

Beyond the Laboratory

Truth Explosion: We can carry on the work of God's kingdom.

Match each worker with the kind of job he or she does.

1. firefighter

2. cashier

3. restaurant server

4. mail carrier

5. police officer

6. snake milker

7. professional mourner

8. dog food taster

9. fortune cookie writer

10. professional apologizer

a. extracts venom from poisonous snakes

b. brings packages and mail to specific addresses

c. gets paid to tell people someone else is sorry

d. tests the quality and flavor of dog food

e. protects and serves the public

f. delivers food and drinks that people order

g. writes the sayings inside Chinese fortune cookies

h. extinguishes fires in buildings

i. gets paid to attend funerals and mourn for strangers

j. helps people purchase food and other items

What kind of work does a "witness for Christ" do? Use the space below to write a job description, qualifications, and benefits for such a position.

Answers: h, j, f, b, e, a, i, d, g, c

Don't Rub Me the Wrong Way

Topic: Getting along
Time: 15–20 minutes
Group Size: Small groups
Mess Meter: **1** 2 3

God has called us to live in peace.
—1 Corinthians 7:15

Formula for Success

- 2 coffee cans with tight-fitting lids
- sand
- 2 thermometers
- timer *(optional)*

Sibling rivalry is a lot like friction. The hotter things get, the more you fight! Kids get to shake things up and check out what happens when molecules collide.

Truth Explosion: We can live in peace with each other.

Kids love this experiment because they get to compete against each other and be as wiggly as they want! As they shake up the friction in two coffee cans of sand, they will measure the heat generated by their frenzied motion.

Let's take a quick poll. Who in here is the oldest child in your family? Who is the youngest? Somewhere in the middle? Take a count of each group. **We all know it's hard to live with brothers and sisters—especially when everyone wants his or her own way. *Friction* is the term describing two things rubbing against each other. Let's see just how hot families can get when brothers and sisters start to rub each other the wrong way.**

Assign kids to two or more teams. You might want to divide by birth order position or some other division. Each team gets a coffee can filled about two-thirds of the way with clean sand. Before starting, each side takes the resting temperature of its sand by slipping a thermometer in the center of the can (don't let the bulb touch the sides). Record this temperature.

Romans 12:16–18; 1 Peter 3:8

The teams will have three minutes to shake their cans as furiously as they can. They can toss it back and forth, shake it up and down, or roll it along the ground, taking care not to let any sand escape. Set a ticking timer to make the competition more suspenseful!

When time's up, each team will take the temperature of its agitated can of sand. They will probably even be able to feel the difference! The team that created the most heat in its coffee can of sand is declared the winner!

Lab Results

- **What other things cause heat when they rub together?** (Car engines, matches, and even cold hands become warmer when different parts rub together.)
- **Why is learning to live peacefully—and not heated up—with a brother and sister good training for the rest of your life?** (It will teach you self-control with others. God wants us to live in harmony with others.)
- **Sometimes the other person tries to create conflict even when we don't want to. What should you do then?** (It's best to either separate yourself from the situation for a time or try to soften them with a kind word. If that doesn't work, ask an adult to help you come to a compromise.)

Super Science Fact

Friction—the rapid collision of molecules—always results in heat. Mechanical energy—movement and friction—can transfer to thermal energy (heat).

Beyond the Laboratory

Truth Explosion: We can live in peace with each other.

Live in peace with your brothers and sisters.

1. There are at least five or six really hard things God tells us to do in Romans 12:16–18. What are they? Write them down here.

2. Read 1 Peter 3:8–11. This passage repeats some of the instructions from Romans. What are at least four new things that this passage commands us to do?

3. Write the names of brothers or sisters you have. If you are an only child, write the names of friends, cousins, aunts, or uncles.

What are two things you could say to these people that would brighten their day?

Just for Fun: Put a little bit of the warm sand from your team's coffee can into a tiny plastic zip-top bag to take home. Write down one of the Scripture references above on the front of the bag with a permanent marker. Tack it up in your room as a reminder to keep cool when things heat up!

Strike! You're Out!

Topic: Gentleness
Time: 15–20 minutes
Group Size: Small groups
Mess Meter: 1 **2** 3

Formula for Success

- cornstarch
- water
- shallow bowl

The properties of cornstarch can be a little like "movie quicksand." Is it a solid or a liquid? Making a simple mixture of cornstarch and water illustrates how a gentle touch can ironically be more effective than a rough strike.

Truth Explosion: We can be gentle.

Let your gentleness be evident to all.
—Philippians 4:5

Note: You might want to prepare this experiment ahead of time, to see how different-sized bowls work to create the "quicksand" effect.

Suppose I have got a piece of concrete on the side of my house I want to get rid of. How do you think I get down to the dirt hiding underneath? Any ideas? Listen to kids' suggestions. Some may say use a sledgehammer or a jackhammer like they've seen at construction sites. Some might tell you to hire a crew to crack it open.

Would you think I was crazy if I said I was going to brush across that concrete with a broom instead? How about blowing on it with some gentle air? Would that work? Maybe I could take a soft sponge and wipe it gently?

Of course that won't work. Only the hard blows of a heavy object will be able to break apart a thick material like concrete. That only makes good sense. But what if I told you that sometimes a gentle touch can be more effective than a hard strike? Is that possible? Let's try to figure it out with another experiment.

Pour about two cups of cornstarch into a shallow pan, maybe two or three inches deep. Add just enough water to dissolve the cornstarch into a fluid appearance. Don't let kids touch or stir the mixture just yet. Part of the fun is seeing their reaction to the peculiar properties of this "liquid."

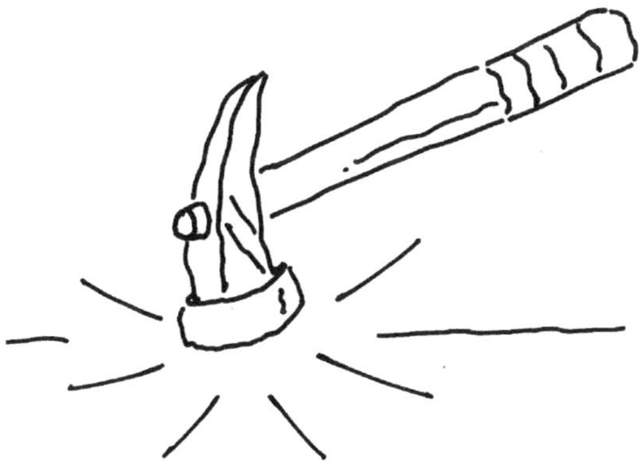

Proverbs 25:15; 1 Corinthians 4:21; Ephesians 4:2

One by one, I'd like you to put your finger gently into the mixture and see if you can touch the bottom of the bowl. Kids should have little trouble poking a finger into the mixture and feeling the bottom of the bowl. They will no doubt react to the strange "feeling" of this mixture.

This time, instead of poking a gentle finger into the mix, I want you to use your hand to pound the surface to get to the bottom of the bowl. Surprisingly, kids will not be able to reach the bottom by using this "strike and pound" method.

Lab Results

- **In the case of breaking up concrete, obviously we need a hard strike or blow to get to the bottom. But today, we saw that sometimes a soft touch is more effective. What kinds of situations in your life might require you to be softer rather than harder?** Listen to students' ideas. For example, sometimes teachers can get more out of a student by being gentle in their approach to learning, or a house pet might be more willing to come to the person who has a peaceful temperament.
- **What do the words *meek* and *humble* mean?** You might want to place synonyms for these on a whiteboard or poster.
- **Sometimes God wants us to take a forceful approach to a situation, such as confronting a wrong or standing up for the weak. Other times He asks us to have a humble, meek spirit. Let's have some volunteers read the following Bible verses out loud.** Have several of your students look up these verses to share with the group: Proverbs 25:15; Matthew 5:5; Ephesians 4:2.

Super Science Fact

Rheology is the study of condensed matter that can "flow" in certain circumstances. When pressure is applied to the long molecules in cornstarch, the material reacts like a solid.

Beyond the Laboratory

Truth Explosion: We can be gentle.

There are ten situations listed at the bottom of the page and space for you to add your own. Copy them into one of the two columns below.

Needs the power of a gentle spirit!	Needs the power of a resolute spirit!

1. My friend has a stomachache because of a low test score.
2. I'm tempted to lie to my mother.
3. the class bully picks on my best friend.
4. My little sister had her bike stolen from the park.
5. I get jealous of my friends' expensive things.
6. Kids at school don't believe God cares for them.
7. I made the volleyball team, but my friend didn't.
8. No one wants to be friends with the special education kids at school.
9. I'm too busy to memorize Bible verses.
10. My dad lost his job today.

What other scenarios can you think of?

ChemiCool!

Topic: Love
Time: 20 minutes to begin forming
Group Size: Large group
Mess Meter: 1 **2** 3

Love is patient, love is kind. It does not envy, it does not boast, it is not proud.
—1 Corinthians 13:4

Formula for Success

- 6 charcoal briquettes
- shallow bowl
- salt
- laundry bluing (look in the laundry section of your store or ask your grocer)
- water
- ammonia
- food coloring
- tablespoons
- wiggle eyes, glue *(optional)*

Love is a basic life need and the very nature of God. As this chemical experiment grows it will show your kids how to grow and grow in love.

Truth Explosion: We can love others.

If you cannot find laundry bluing to perform this experiment, it can be done without it. The result, however, will not be as striking.

Place the briquettes in a bowl. **Let's say these charcoal briquettes are my six little buddies. Who will give my buddies a hand?**

Have kids glue wiggly eyes on the briquettes.
My buddies seem like a pretty close group. They sit in the same school bus every morning. They see each other in class just about every day and they eat cheeseburgers in the cafeteria at lunchtime. But … because my buddies don't take the time to know one another they can't ever become devoted, caring friends. Let's change that!

What would be a great way to start a conversation with someone new?

How can a soccer team on the playground show a new teammate that he or she belongs?

When my buddies see how much they have in common, a loving friendship is sure to grow. Let's see our buddies grow in love!

Have kids mix six tablespoons of salt, six tablespoons of laundry bluing, six tablespoons of water, and one tablespoon of ammonia and spoon it over the briquettes. Also drop some colorful food coloring on top of each of the briquettes. Wait. In 20 minutes or so, small crystals will begin to form on the charcoal. (Beware: This experiment is an assault on the nose. In other words, it stinks! But the end product is well worth it.) On day two, be sure to sprinkle on more salt.

Lab Results

- **Why are kids afraid to reach out in friendship to someone new? How can a group of loving friends change that?** (Kids may be afraid of being rejected or make fun of. If you have friends who love you the way you are, you'll be more confident in reaching out to others and accepting them as they are too.)

Super Science Fact

As the water evaporates on the charcoal surfaces, deposits of solids are left behind, forming crystals. Crystals are also formed as the solution is drawn up into the porous charcoal, a process known as capillary action.

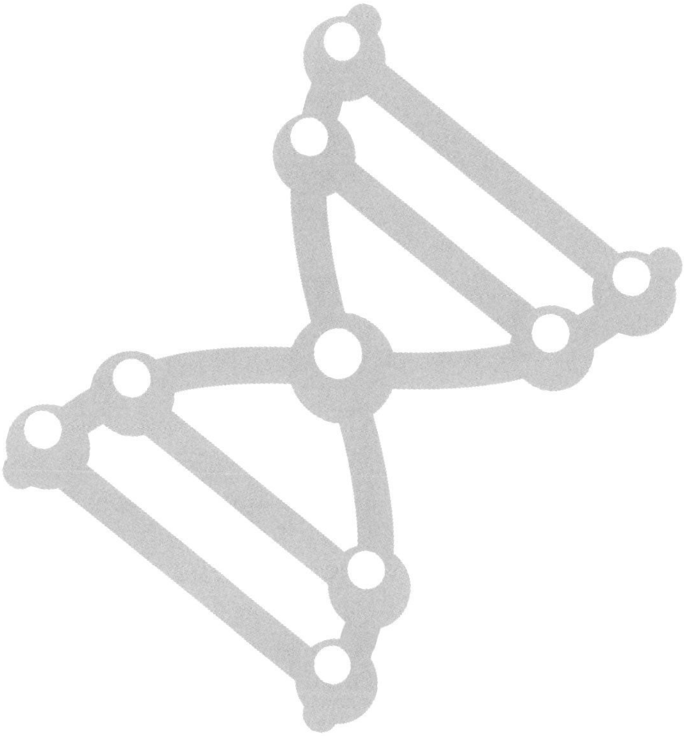

Beyond the Laboratory

Truth Explosion: We can love others.

Practice saying, "I love you" in each of these languages:

Spanish: *Te amo*

Chinese: *Wo ai ni*

French: *Je t'aime*

Swahili: *Naku penda*

There are many other ways to express love, other than with words. In the space below, list some ways that you can SHOW love to those around you.

IN MY FAMILY

AT MY SCHOOL

IN MY NEIGHBORHOOD

ON MY TEAM

AT MY CHURCH

Humility on the Rise

Topic: Humility
Time: 15 minutes
Group Size: Whole class or small groups
Mess Meter: **1** 2 3

Do nothing out of selfish ambition or vain conceit. Rather, in humility value others above yourselves, not looking to your own interests but each of you to the interests of the others.
—Philippians 2:3–4

Formula for Success

- brightly-colored golf ball
- smiley-face sticker
- uncooked rice
- wide-mouth jar with lid

See humility in your kids without lifting a finger!

Truth Explosion: We can think of others before ourselves.

If you have a large class, prepare several sets of supplies so everyone can have a close look.

When is it difficult for you to place the needs of others before your own? (when I'd rather be playing on the computer or eating a snack; when kids are mean or selfish to me)

Have kids gather around you as you set the jar on a table. Place the smiley-face sticker on the golf ball and then gently place the ball inside the jar. **Hello, Mr. Humility! Mr. Humility reminds us that when we humble ourselves we think of others first.** Have students take turns pouring small amounts of dry rice on top of the golf ball. Keep adding rice until the ball is covered by 3" or more. Be sure to allow 1½" of space at the top of the jar.

Screw on the jar lid. Ask a volunteer to hold the jar and move or "stir" it from side to side (not up and down) without lifting it from the table. Watch what happens! In no time, the golf ball rises and rests neatly on the surface of the rice. Remove the lid.

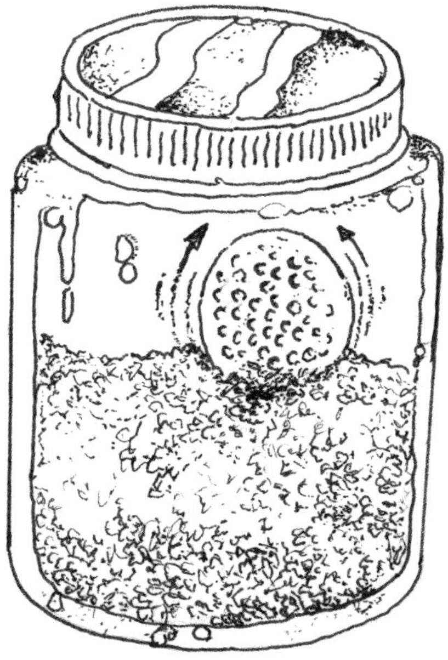

Without lifting a finger … I mean, the jar … we saw Mr. Humility rise above the busyness and frustrations of his own life to willingly serve others—all with a smile!

Repeat the experiment until everyone has a chance to try it.

Jesus humbled himself when He came to Earth to live. Although divine and holy and without sin, He humbled himself and died on a cross. In His humility, Jesus showed how much He cares for you and me.

Lab Results

- **What example of humility does Jesus give us?** (He humbled himself enough to die for us.)

- **Name two ways you could humble yourself at home.** (Choose a household job no one likes to do—clean the kitty litter box and do it without complaint; agree to shower last on a school morning; read to a younger brother or sister even if you're just dying to lace up your soccer spikes and head for the field!)

- **How does a humble attitude show brothers and sisters, family and friends that you care?** (When we value the things others want and need more than we value what we want and need, it shows those people are important to us.)

Super Science Fact

Two things cannot occupy the same space at the same time. Shaking or stirring the jar forces the grains of rice closer together. This pressure pushes the golf ball to the surface.

Beyond the Laboratory

Truth Explosion: We can think of others before ourselves.

Complete the following sentences in ways that show humility. If you have trouble, think about what Jesus would do.

1. You just nailed a double in your team's championship baseball game, sending in the winning run. As your whole team runs over to congratulate you, you say:

2. You're sitting at lunch and notice that the girl next to you doesn't have anything to eat, while you've got plenty. You decide to:

3. You are in the middle of your favorite video game and are about to beat your high score! Just then your mom pulls up in the van and needs help carrying in the groceries. You:

4. You're in a fast food restaurant, and you watch as an older man stumbles and spills his entire tray. You choose to:

5. You've been saving for months to get a new set of headphones, and you finally have enough. But on the way to the store, you pass a homeless woman and her kids. You:

Being humble doesn't mean you let other people mistreat you or you ignore your own needs. Being humble means you are strong enough to say no to some of the things you want in order to give someone else what they need. Ask God to help you grow in humility—and in love.

Get Away from Me!

Topic: Attitudes
Time: 15–20 minutes
Group Size: Small groups
Mess Meter: **1** 2 3

Live in harmony with one another.
—Romans 12:16

Formula for Success

- empty aluminum can
- balloon
- plastic comb
- tissue paper

Have you ever seen a balloon move a soda can? Can a comb ever be too "pushy"? Discovering how static electricity can repel objects reveals the truth about a bad attitude toward others.

Truth Explosion: We can have a Christlike attitude.

While God doesn't expect us to have artificial or insincere sweetness, He does command us to show love and compassion toward others. Our attitudes make us attractive messengers of the gospel, just as a grumpy spirit will naturally push others away.

What if I told you I could move this soda can without touching it at all? What if I couldn't blow air on it, push it, or touch the surface in any way? Do you think I could do it? Let kids try to come up with ideas.

You'll see how I'm going to do it, but first I need a volunteer to blow up this balloon. Choose a student. **While he or she is inflating this balloon, let me ask you a question: Anybody here like to hang around grumpy people? What about negative, angry, growl-in-your-face people? Of course not! It's in our nature to move away from sour attitudes and mean hearts. But we're attracted to the kindness and gentleness of others.**

Take the inflated balloon and rub the balloon back and forth across another volunteer's hair several times. Hold the balloon about three to four centimeters away from an aluminum can placed on

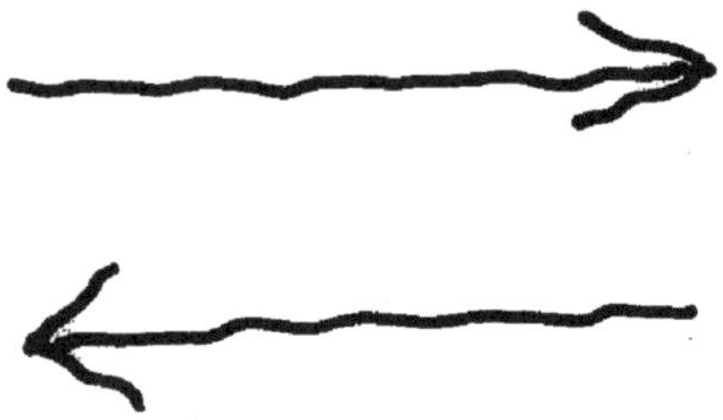

Philippians 2:2–4; 1 Peter 3:8–9

its side. Slowly move the balloon farther away. The can will either follow the balloon or be repelled by it. Either way, it will move.

In another similar experiment, have a student pass a plastic comb through his or her hair several times. Wave it over a pile of small, loosely-torn pieces of tissue paper. The charged electrical particles created on the comb will attract the loose tissue.

Lab Results

- **Have you ever gotten a brief electrical shock from touching someone or something? Why do you think that happens?** (Kids may recall experiences like being on a metal slide at the playground or touching a doorknob after walking across a carpet. Explain that friction has caused a build-up of charged particles. Protons are the positively charged particles while electrons have a negative charge.)

- **Just as our aluminum soda can was repelled by the balloon, sometimes we get a build-up of negativity in our attitude. It's no surprise we push people away! After all, who wants to put up with that? What kind of people are you drawn to?** Listen to kids' responses.

- **Does this mean we have to pretend to be happy all the time? Of course not! Listen to this Bible passage from Ephesians 4:2–3: "Be completely humble and gentle; be patient, bearing with one another in love. Make every effort to keep the unity of the Spirit through the bond of peace."**

Super Science Fact

Static electricity is caused by the transfer of electrons from one object to another—sometimes through friction. Similar charges (positive or negative) repel each other. Opposite charges attract each other.

Beyond the Laboratory

Truth Explosion: We can have a Christlike attitude.

Find the following words in the puzzle: grumpy, angry, bitter, negative, sour, sarcastic, forgiving, kind, soft, understanding, humble, tense, reasonable, selfish, respectful.

F	A	B	E	L	B	A	N	O	S	A	E	R	C	L
R	G	W	S	A	R	C	A	S	T	I	C	V	P	A
E	U	R	O	S	P	A	W	C	Y	I	O	D	U	G
S	L	L	U	G	S	N	J	A	O	A	B	N	N	K
P	O	R	R	M	R	G	D	E	L	Y	N	I	D	T
E	K	T	R	M	P	R	I	M	O	G	V	G	E	G
C	I	R	D	F	F	Y	G	B	I	T	T	E	R	H
T	N	E	G	A	T	I	V	E	J	Z	X	C	S	Y
F	D	T	V	B	P	T	F	N	H	M	A	S	T	D
U	F	T	E	N	S	E	H	S	J	T	K	L	A	Q
L	W	I	E	R	T	U	I	I	F	O	P	L	N	K
J	H	B	G	F	D	F	S	O	A	A	Z	X	D	C
R	H	U	M	B	L	E	S	A	M	N	B	V	I	C
R	K	L	N	E	A	F	O	R	G	I	V	I	N	G
W	E	E	S	A	I	O	Y	T	T	W	C	M	G	L

When you find a word, jot it down in either the REPEL or ATTRACT column.

REPEL **ATTRACT**

Little Things Make a Big Impact

Topic: Making a difference
Time: 15–20 minutes
Group Size: Small groups
Mess Meter: 1 2 **3**

Have I not commanded you? Be strong and courageous. Do not be afraid; do not be discouraged, for the LORD your God will be with you wherever you go.
—Joshua 1:9

Formula for Success

- heavy-duty zip-top sandwich bag
- 1 cup of water
- 6" paper towel square
- 2 tablespoons of baking soda
- ½ cup of vinegar

Kids don't always feel like they have much of an impact. By making a sandwich bag "bomb," they see that even little things can make a bang!

Truth Explosion: We can shake up the world!

Kids may not feel old enough to be independent, strong enough to complete powerful tasks, or big enough to tackle the world quite yet. This experiment illustrates the power a very small package can create.

This experiment requires practice ahead of time, so test it out in your at home before you try it with your group. You may need to stroke the side of the bag with a few rubs of coarse sandpaper to weaken it enough to explode. Plan to "blow up" several bags. In the event none of them pop, kids can kick them back and forth until one of the bags does its thing!

We're going to shake things up a little bit today by making a homemade sandwich bag "bomb." Don't worry—it won't create any fiery explosions. But the gas created in our plastic bag will have nowhere to go except out! You'll find out that the most ordinary ingredients in your kitchen can be a lot stronger than they look.

It's important to check for leaks in the bag before you begin. Perhaps you can have one or two kids test the bag first by filling it with a few cups of water, then sealing it carefully. When you're sure there are no leaks, pour out the water.

Place two tablespoons of baking soda in the center of your paper towel square. Fold one-third of the towel over the center and then repeat with the other side. Fold the two ends to the center, creating a little packet. The trick to this experiment is not letting

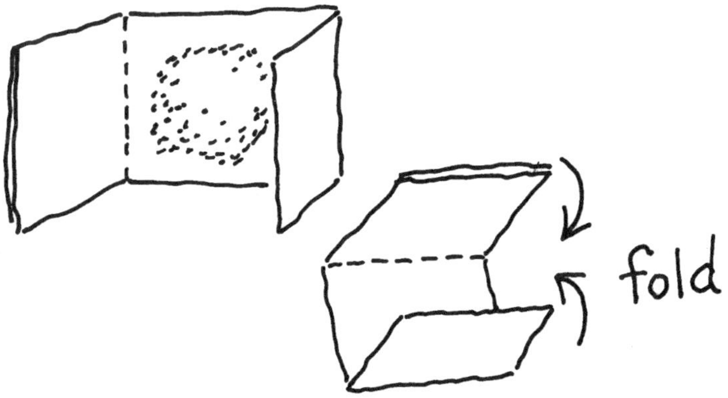

1 Timothy 4:12; 1 John 2:14

the vinegar mixture touch the paper towel until right before you want it to pop. You can do this by pouring one-half cup of water and one-fourth cup of vinegar into the bag first. Then have someone place the paper towel packet inside the bag and grip it from the outside. Pinch the baking soda packet against the dry part of the bag, making sure to keep it well above the liquid. Seal the top zipper. Continue to pinch the packet from the outside of the bag as you carry the experiment outside to an open area.

Shake the bag, let go of the packet, and toss everything on the ground. The air inside the bag will expand quickly, and with nowhere to go, it will inflate against the weakest part of the bag—most likely the top seal. In a few seconds—POP! Your sandwich bag bomb has been detonated!

Lab Results

- **Why do you think we couldn't let the baking soda touch the water mixture at the beginning of this experiment?** (The air in the bag would have started to expand right away before we had time to seal it.)
- **If we put plain baking soda in a sealed bag, what would have happened?** (Nothing, because it needed the other ingredients to make a reaction.)
- **By ourselves, we're not that powerful. What happens when God comes into our lives? How is this a little bit like this experiment?** (When God comes into our lives, we are able to impact the world in a much bigger way. He gives us strength and helps us make a BANG!)
- **Repeat after me this verse from Psalm 89:13: Your arm is endued with power.** Kids repeat. **Your hand is strong.** Kids repeat. **Your right hand is exalted.** Kids repeat.

Super Science Fact

Carbon dioxide is formed when water and baking soda combine. Unlike other "bombs" that use fiery explosions, this one would actually put out a fire. In fact, if you lower a match into the bag after it pops, it will go out!

Beyond the Laboratory

Truth Explosion: We can shake up the world!

Work with a friend or two and answer these questions.

1. Have you ever heard about kids doing some pretty important things? What did they do? Write your answers together.

2. Find 1 Timothy 4:12. Choose someone in your group to read the verse out loud. What are the five things this verse says we can do to set a good example for others?

   1. ______________________________
   2. ______________________________
   3. ______________________________
   4. ______________________________
   5. ______________________________

3. For each of the words above, write something you can do that brings honor to God.

   1. ______________________________
   2. ______________________________
   3. ______________________________
   4. ______________________________
   5. ______________________________

4. Rewrite the verse below, but put your name in place of the underlined words. Read it out loud to a partner, and then let your partner read his or her version back to you!

"I write to you, young men, because you are strong, and the word of God lives in you, and you have overcome the evil one" (1 John 2:14).

5. Who is "the evil one"? Does he have any power over you?

6. What is a good way to let the Word of God live in you?

Scripture Index

Old Testament

New Testament

Topic Index

Lab Notes

Lab Notes

Lab Notes

Lab Notes

Lab Notes

Lab Notes